Spiritual Treasure

Paraphrases of Spiritual Classics

Bernard Bangley

PAULIST PRESS
New York/Mahwah

Library of Congress
Catalog Card Number: 84-61026

ISBN: 0-8091-2646-X

Published by Paulist Press
997 Macarthur Boulevard
Mahwah, New Jersey 07430

Printed and bound in the
United States of America

CONTENTS

ACKNOWLEDGEMENT

All Scripture quotations are from the Authorized Version, except for those marked with an asterisk, which are paraphrased by the author.

Gratitude is expressed to Kathryn Lewis and Charlotte Stone for their careful preparation of the final manuscript.

Spiritual Treasure

INTRODUCTION

It is possible to know God personally. There can be a relationship of love between an individual mortal and the Sustainer of the universe. The human soul is capable of living dialogue with the Almighty. Loving communication of this sort will have a tremendous effect upon one's attitude toward and relationship with other people. These are the unanimous conclusions of men and women of many nationalities throughout the twenty centuries that separate us from the days of the New Testament.

From kitchen helper to court nobleman, the humble reporters of the spiritual life come from all degrees of social rank. Whether the experiences are described in the erotic language of aroused Spanish blood or in the elegant propriety of cultured French, each writer corroborates the other. They ransack the storehouses of a maturing Latin or a newly-born English to find appropriate words with which to express their experiences. They complain of inadequate metaphors and caution against misinterpretation. They face the discouraging incredulity of religious professionals and deal with open opposition. They insist that it is all God's free gift, that everyone possesses the capacity, and that unsophisticated faith is the key that unlocks the greatest treasure chest in all creation. To the skeptical they can only say, "Try it yourself and see."

The record of their discoveries is far more than a valuable antique. It is a lively guide for those who follow the same path. Today, as in every generation, there are individuals who, in spite of themselves, arrive at parallel conclusions. Sometimes these contemporary souls are fully conscious of those who have previously taken off their shoes before the burning bush. Others may stumble into the Holy of Holies unannounced and almost independently. Such an experience usually brings with it a curious mixture of doubts and uncertainties. As Dante needed Virgil to guide him on his way through unknown realms, so we need to

take hold of another hand in our own spiritual pilgrimage. It is impera-
tive that we sit down quietly with another who understands the terror and
the joy, the fire and the cloud, the bright light and the dark night. The
writings of Christians who passed this way before we were born are
therefore invaluable. We call their books "classics" not because they
are old, but because they are timeless in nature and of lasting value to
our tribe.

It is an impressive fact that these authors are well integrated,
healthy, productive personalities. The collective achievement of the persons represented in these pages is considerable. Many of them are the
outstanding individuals of their time. Secular history cannot be written
without giving them their due credit. Apparently there is something of
practical value in the mystical experience, something that allows God to
work through us. Each one describes a sensation of being caught up in
God. The transformed moment is in itself a private moment, but it never
ends there. The point is made over and over that any love of God that
does not result in an overwhelming love of neighbor is an unhealthy
love. There is no seeking after a private display of divine pyrotechnics
to be enjoyed in isolation from one's relation to the world. There were,
and there are, groups and movements which offer personal entertainment and diversion, but mainline Christian mysticism is not among
them. The experience of adoration sends the Christian out among others,
fortified for service.

To cite as examples the lives in this book is to demonstrate that
such service is often harsh and demanding. A less spiritual person might
easily fail under such pressures. It is startling to realize how much of the
best Christian literature has been written in jail. Think of some of the letters of the Apostle Paul, the voluminous output of St. John of the
Cross, Bunyan's *The Pilgrim's Progress,* Bonhoeffer's writings, and
King's *Letter from a Birmingham Jail.* To be in love with God is de-
monstrably hazardous. We may hear dedicated Christians speak of
"quiet rest," but the words always need interpretation.

Morton Kelsey has compared the Church with a transformer which
reduces high voltage spirituality to ordinary house current. In general
application some domestication of the divine is certainly necessary. Dy-
namite is not sold to the general public. And with good reason. It is dangerous. One needs to know how to handle such power. There must be a

constructive application. It is understandable that leaders of the Church have tended to insulate us from direct exposure to the holy. Outstanding Christians have been nurtured with the rituals of public worship and devotional handbooks. Many are content with singing a hymn, repeating a prayer, and hearing a passage of Scripture expounded.

But sometimes God reaches across commonplace piety and touches a person in a disturbingly intimate way. As this book was going into its final draft I received a letter from an out-of-state visitor to the church I pastor. He said that he wanted to express special appreciation for a particular message. "Sermons have seldom affected me as this one did. I am at a loss to tell if the effect was mystical, spiritual, intellectual, inspirational, or some combination of these and other unrecognized factors. It was of great help to me and I will long remember and benefit from it." That sermon was nothing more than a meditation upon the three appearances of Thomas in the Gospel of John. It will never make it into a volume of "great sermons." But as the businessman-visitor focused on the images I suggested, a curtain was drawn aside for him and he experienced something that would make every author in this book smile and nod knowingly.

It has become clear that an intellectual approach to religion needs to be counterbalanced by the spiritual. It is somewhat amusing to see how even the renaissance of spirituality can be shielded like an isotope in lead by the pedagogues. The writers in these pages, and all their kin, can now be measured on apophatic/kataphatic and speculative/affective scales! This can be an interesting exercise, provided it does not obscure the content of the works. Still, one wonders just how Brother Lawrence would respond if a reporter were to ask him whether he were apophatic or kataphatic.

Purpose, Style, and Sources

These paraphrases were not prepared by a credentialed scholar for the edification of other scholars. They are the product of a busy pastor who is attempting to communicate the vast treasures of our faith to an audience that is familiar with little more than the titles.

My dedication to this "hobby" began about seven years ago when I started to work on *The Imitation of Christ*. That effort has been published under the title, *Growing in His Image*.[1] One thing led to another.

Twenty-two years of ministry have taught me that people become most interested if I talk about something that honestly interests me. Enthusiasm is contagious. As a forum for sharing exciting discoveries, I instituted "Breakfast with the Pastor" and scheduled it for Saturday mornings at eight. I solemnly promised to let everyone out at nine whether I was finished or not. In addition to the condensations in this anthology I also presented *The Divine Comedy* with slides of the Doré engravings, rendered Cicero's "On Growing Old" as a modern talk, and examined the *Aeneid* for its influences on Christianity. I took them through *The Pilgrim's Progress* and *The Testament of Devotion*. I had expected about thirty people to show up. More than three hundred attended regularly. It became necessary to repeat the same material on successive Saturdays in order to accommodate the crowds. Many listeners to my "talking books" would never have read these works for themselves. And yet, after this oral introduction, some of them turned to the original books with keen interest.

We are living in an era when oral literature is returning to favor. Television, films and music are training our popular culture to absorb spoken ideas. Guigo II, in his *The Ladder of Monks,* said: "Listening is a form of reading. We say we have read both those books we have actually read and also the ones which our teachers have read to us."

My purpose, then, was to prepare honestly representative condensations that could be read aloud to the uninitiated in less than an hour. I wanted them to be enjoyed by the growing percentage of modern readers who lack the time, skill, and motivation to tackle these classics in their complete versions. This was not an easy assignment. There were failures. I could not begin to do justice to St. John of the Cross or Julian of Norwich. I read them avidly, but there seemed to be no way to paraphrase them adequately. On the other hand, some of the works literally took hold of me. The writing was all joy.

To fulfill my purpose, I sought a style that was similar to each author's, but at the same time natural to modern ears and eyes. Style is the stumbling block for all but the most literate. Earlier generations wrote long, complicated sentences. Repetition is commonplace and often involves passages of considerable length. Even Allison Peers, who care-

---

1. Harold Shaw Publishers, Wheaton, Illinois (1983).

fully translated every word of St. Teresa of Avila and St. John of the Cross, admits that such writing could be improved if it were cut by a third.[2]

If the older style of writing is cumbersome and confusing to the vast majority of today's reading public, it is even less expedient for oral delivery. Streamlining and simplification are therefore primary requirements. Still, it is important to be sensitive to shades of meaning and word-play in the original languages. Both the character of the work and its message frequently depend upon subtleties. An appreciation of St. Teresa, for example, requires an awareness of her clever handling of Spanish. Footnotes call attention to many such details.

The peculiar kind of paraphrasing that produces oral literature sometimes demands that an entire page be reduced to a single sentence. This can be disconcerting to those who are familiar with the original work. It can also be dangerous. A marginal notation in another hand on the first page of the autograph of St. Teresa's *Interior Castle* says: "Request with love that whoever reads this book respect the words and letters written by such a holy hand. Try to understand her and you will discover that no editing is necessary. If you cannot understand her, give her credit for knowing what she wrote. Don't attempt to change any of her words. If you are not able to grasp her meaning, you will think that what she has said very properly is actually improper. This is the way editors destroy books."

Because I was aware of the hazards, careful study preceded each paraphrase. It must not be assumed, however, that they are the result of painstaking examinations of original texts. Such a task is beyond my competency. Of the titles included in this volume, the only original language sources available to me were of St. Augustine's *Confessions*. Two editions were especially valuable. *The Confessions of Augustine,* edited by John Gibb and William Montgomery (Cambridge: University Press, 1927) is a complete basic source. There are some extremely helpful notes in the selections taken from Books I–IX by James Marshall Campbell and Martin R. P. McGuire (New York: Prentice-Hall, 1931).

---

2. As an interesting sidelight, notice that St. Augustine condensed himself. In Book Nine, Chapter VIII of his *Confessions* we read: "I omit many things, for I must make haste. O God, accept my confession and my gratitude for countless things not mentioned."

Beyond this, my basic approach was to read everything I could find in English. I used my annual study leave for research. Many books were borrowed by mail from cooperating libraries. Not a few were purchased and became a part of my personal collection. The brief bibliographies are intended only as guides for the uninitiated. They suggest books that are commonly available in English for general readers. These lists represent a fraction of my homework. For instance, a truly fabulous source for St. Francis is *St. Francis of Assisi, Writings and Early Biographies: English Omnibus of the Sources for the Life of St. Francis,* edited by Marion A. Habig (Chicago: Franciscan Herald, 1973). It is a bulky volume that is difficult to find.

One additional guideline is behind each of these paraphrases. It is my desire that these scraps should give a fair impression of the whole. Collections of inspirational quotations torn from great works have their place, but that is not my design. Most of these works present carefully developed continuous thought.

It seems to me that even a brief paraphrase can give a clear indication of the larger structure. The author of a deserving work not represented here, *The Cloud of Unknowing,* made this statement at the beginning and end of his book: ''I charge you with the authority of love, if anyone reads this book for himself or to others, or copies it, or listens to it read, be sure to read it all—straight through. It may be that there is something in the beginning or in the middle which depends upon full exposition later. If one were to examine one part while neglecting the other, he could easily be led astray.''

With one exception, nothing has been transposed.[3] Everything flows in its natural order and sequence. Parenthetical notations clearly indicate where I have ignored intrusive chapter headings. Omitted sections are briefly summarized. My intention is to give a potential new reader an adequate preview of what is waiting to be enjoyed in the original works. Two authors, St. Francis and Fénelon, did not leave us a particular title that could be worked through in the manner of the others. For these it is necessary to pull together shorter pieces. The former left precious little in writing; the latter, quite a lot.

---

3. St. Augustine, *Confessions.* Book Six, Chapter VIII, is inserted inside Chapter VII for continuity.

An Observation on Favorite Scripture

The more widely one reads in this literature, the more evident it becomes that there are two portions of Scripture that can be depended upon to strike sympathetic chords in each author. In the New Testament, the incident of Mary and Martha is by far the most popular. The introduction to *Interior Castle* will have more to say on this.

Among the Old Testament books, *The Song of Songs* is a decided favorite. Few modern scholars are able to see anything in this love poem that says anything about "mystical marriage." Marvin Pope, in his massive Anchor Bible volume, defers to an older commentary by Paschal Parente when it becomes necessary to recall this earlier widespread allegorical interpretation. For our purposes, it is only necessary that we understand that the experienced relationship between the human soul and God can find no better metaphor than that of lovers. When the uninitiated read the passionate poetry of St. John of the Cross they wonder that it can have anything to do with religion. It is as juicy as *The Song of Songs*. We may frown upon what some would call "misinterpretation" of this beautiful book, but we must concede that the writers included herein saw something in it that harmonized with their state of soul. "Oh, what precious pearls!" St. John of the Cross exclaimed when he heard it read by his deathbed.

God is love. To know him is to be in love. Our soul becomes the bride and Christ the groom. The mystics are trying to tell us it is something like that, and if we would be open to the indwelling of that love, we would find it out for ourselves.

AUGUSTINE: CONFESSION

St. Augustine's *Confession* is one of the great treasures of the Christian Church. It is in a class with Michelangelo's Pietà and Bach's *St. Matthew Passion*. The book was written in the year 399 when the author was in his mid-forties.

Augustine was born in Thagaste, a Roman city in North Africa, on November 13, 354. He will tell his own life story in the pages that follow—the first extensive autobiography in the literature of the world. Later, he became Bishop of Hippo (again, in North Africa) and remained in this administrative position for three and a half decades until his death in 430. He was a man of considerable intellectual ability and served the Church well during a time of upheaval and rampant heresy. His clear thinking remained an important guide for Christianity for many centuries.

Since the young man Augustine was a Manichean, the reader of his *Confession* needs to know at least a few basic facts regarding the movement. It was founded by a Babylonian named Mani[1] a little more than a hundred years before Augustine was born. Mani had gleaned ideas from a wide variety of religions and brought them together in a system of his own. As a gnostic faith, Manicheism claimed to be both inspired and rational. That it was neither will become clear to a reader of the *Confession*.

There is a beauty in this book that even the best translations fail to convey. Augustine was a master craftsman with words and he used his powers to bring a diversity of appropriate styles to his work which can only be hinted at in these pages. If the subject demanded it, he wrote wonderfully sonorous passages of poetic beauty. If he wanted to convey an intense psychological struggle, he wrote in short, breathless sen-

---

1. Sometimes "Manes."

11

tences. Proportion and imagery are precisely correct in every instance. Word-play is common. For instance, when he refers to Carthage as a "cauldron" he uses *Carthago* and *sartago*. The *Confession* still seems to possess the heat of creation. Whenever a reader opens its cover it begins to live and breathe. The people he introduces to us are genuine and believable.

Augustine imposed the form of a direct confession to God upon his life story. It has been called "a 100,000 word act of contrition." The reader is never allowed to forget that he is privy to a personal confession. Every chapter is replete with asides and prayers addressed to God. The author hides nothing. He wrote with an honest sincerity that has the power to shock even modern culture.

He quoted the Bible from memory, and that from early Latin versions. It is almost impossible to indicate each reference to Scripture. His writing is saturated with biblical allusions. A few of the more important direct quotations have been noted, but there is a difference of opinion regarding exactly which chapter and verse he meant even in some of these.

CONFESSION

I.

"Great is the Lord, and greatly to be praised . . ." (Ps. 48:1) We are only a fraction of your enormous creation, Lord, but we still want to praise you. You have made us for yourself and our hearts are restless until they rest in you.

Which comes first, knowing you or praying to you? Surely no one can pray to you who does not know you. And yet, maybe we need to pray before we can really know you. "How then shall they call on him in whom they have not believed? and how shall they believe in him of whom they have not heard? and how shall they hear without a preacher?" (Rom. 10:14) My faith, the faith you infused in me, Lord, cries out to you.

O God, you are the greatest and the best,
the strongest,
the most merciful and just,
absolutely concealed and absolutely present,

beautiful,
mysterious,
never changing, but changing everything,
never new; never old,
always in action; always at rest,
attracting all things to yourself, but needing none.
Preserving and fulfilling and sheltering,
conceiving and nourishing and ripening,
continually seeking, but lacking nothing,
you love without the confusion of emotion,
you are jealous, but without fear.
You owe us nothing and yet you give to us as though you were indebted
    to us.
You forgive what is due you, and yet lose nothing yourself.

And after all of this, what have I said? What can anyone say when he speaks of God?

My soul is too small to accommodate you. Enlarge it. It is in ruins. Repair it. I know there are things in it that are offensive to you. " . . . cleanse thou me from secret faults." (Ps. 19:12) I have no desire to deceive myself. "If thou, Lord, shouldst mark iniquities, O Lord, who shall stand?" (Ps. 130:3)

And yet, though I am dust and ashes, let me make a plea for mercy. Tell me a secret, O God. Before I was born, was I anywhere? Did I exist? Where did I come from? I don't know. I only know that you provided for my life from the very first moment of it. It was by your gift that those who nursed me willingly gave me the milk you gave them.

And what were my sins as an infant? Did I cry too impatiently for the breast? Was I self-centered? The innocence of children is the product of an undeveloped body and not the result of a clean mind. I have seen a baby, still too young to talk, seething with jealous anger as it watched another baby at the breast. Innocence is not the word for it when one infant is not able to endure seeing another infant receiving the food upon which life depends. Where or when was I *ever* innocent?

I saw little value in the things I was sent to school to learn. When I failed to study, I was severely beaten. That was when I learned to pray, thinking that you, though unseen, could spare me the beatings at school.

Once I was critically ill. Close to death. My mother was worried and made plans to have me baptized. When I recovered, the baptism was cancelled because they assumed that if I lived I would certainly sin again, and sin after baptism would be a serious matter imperilling my soul. In those days I shared my mother's faith.

Was it wise for them to postpone my baptism? Was it a good thing, my God, for me to be free to sin as I pleased? It would have been far better had I been baptized right then. But my mother knew that I would be subjected to tremendous temptation as I grew out of boyhood, and thought it would be better for those crashing waves to break upon my clay before it was molded in Christ's image.

This I confess to you, O my God: I told many lies. I stole things from my parents. I tried to win games by cheating. I was upset and protested loudly when I caught anyone else doing these things. When *I* was caught, I would rage wildly rather than admit it.

II

As an adolescent, I greatly yearned for all the satisfactions of hell. I became an animal consumed with lust. The only thing I cared about was to love and be loved. Love and lust boiled within me. I went a long way away from you, and you let me go. But you were always with me, touching my pleasures with a little bitterness now and then.

My father called me back from grammar school in Madura to our home in Thagaste. It was his intention to send me to school in Carthage. But because of a lack of money, I had to remain idle at home. The briars of lust overran my garden.

My mother was concerned and begged me not to sin with women—especially not with married women. You were speaking to me through her, and when I ignored her, I ignored you. I heard other boys boasting of their exploits. I did the same thing partly for the pleasure of the act and partly for the pleasure of the boasting. I wanted praise. When I could not equal others in vice, I invented things I had not done.

I began to steal for the joy of stealing. There was a pear tree loaded with fruit. Late one night, a group of us knocked the pears off and carried them away. We never ate them. We did it only because it was fun to do something that was forbidden. I enjoyed evil. Pears were not what my empty soul wanted. I had plenty of pears better than those. It must have been the thrill of breaking God's law. Maybe I enjoyed the companionship of my fellow thieves. We laughed together. There is not much laughter when we are alone. I am sure I would not have stolen those pears if I had been alone. I would not have enjoyed it if others had not participated.

What am I getting at? Who can untangle it? I don't like remembering it.

III.

At the age of sixteen I went to Carthage. That city was a boiling cauldron of forbidden desires. I began to enjoy the theater. The plays mirrored my own miseries and fueled the fires of my heart. I enjoyed being saddened and went looking for things to be sad about. Even the fictitious misery of the actors on stage made me cry. The more my tears flowed the better I liked the drama.

I was studying law, and I intended to be an excellent student. I read books of eloquence with greedy ambition. One of the books I had to study was Cicero's *Hortensius*.[2] It changed my life. As I read it, I saw that the things I vainly treasured were without value. I began to yearn intensely for wisdom.

This was the beginning of my upward journey toward you, O Lord. My father had been dead two years. I was eighteen and my mother was sending me money so I could study eloquence. But I didn't use that book to improve my speech. It was not Cicero's excellent phrasing that reached me; it was what he said. He said that I should love, seek, win, grasp, and embrace Wisdom. This excited me. The only thing missing in those pages was the name of Christ.

So I decided to study the Bible. But the Sacred Scriptures simply didn't make any sense to me. They seemed to me to be far beneath the majesty of Cicero.

Then I began to keep company with the Manicheans, a religious sect that spoke a lot of inflated nonsense. They spoke many of the right words, but they were only noises without meaning. They kept talking to me of "Truth," but they had none.

O my supreme and good Father, Beauty of beauties, O Truth,

---

2. This book has been lost.

Truth, how my soul longed for you when I heard your name spoken! But it was all so many words. They took me in because I thought they spoke with authority. But instead of nourishing me, they starved me. Dreaming of food seems like the real thing, but it will not fill an empty stomach. I ate, but I was not fed.

You raised my soul up out of the dark pit. My mother wept faithfully to you more than mothers weep for dead children. And you heard her, Lord. You heard her. Nine years were to pass. All that time this faithful widow continued her weeping and mourning. She prayed every hour. But for all her efforts, you allowed me to remain in darkness.

You gave her at least two grand assurances. In a dream, you told her that you would be with me. Through a priest, you explained to her that it was pointless to try to argue me out of my errors. I was not yet ready for instruction. I was too excited by the novelty of my heresy. "Leave him alone," he told her. "Only pray to God for him. He will discover by his reading how great is his error. It is not possible that the son of these tears should perish."

IV.

In those years I lived with a woman. We were not married. My wandering eyes picked her out without much care. She was my only woman and I was faithful to her. But there is a great difference between marriage for the sake of children and a lustful relationship that produces unwanted children—though if they are born, we can't help loving them.

I began to teach in my hometown. I had a very dear friend there. We had grown up together. He became seriously ill, and we thought he was going to die. But the fever went away and he recovered. I tried to share a little levity with him, laughing about the way he had been baptized when he was unconscious. He glared at me and said that if I wanted to remain his friend I must not talk like that. This cut me deeply. In a few days the fever returned and he died. I was grief-stricken. I was crushed under a miserable burden which only you, Lord, could lift. But my thoughts about you were fuzzy. My god was my misguided fantasies; not you. When I attempted to place my heavy burden on such vaporous nonsense, it fell through and I was no better than before.

How would I escape myself? Where could I go to avoid me? I decided to leave my hometown, Thagaste, and returned to Carthage.

What is our goal? What are we working so hard to achieve? Go after it if we will, but it is not going to be found where we are looking. We are trying to find good living in a dying world. It is not there. How can there be good living where there is no living?

But I couldn't see this at the time. I was in love with physical beauty. I asked my friends, "Do we love anything other than the beautiful? What, then, is beautiful? What is it that attracts us and gives us pleasure?" It seemed to me that one could distinguish between the beauty of the whole and the beauty of the parts in relation to each other. I wrote two or three books on the Beautiful and the Proper.[3] I've lost them now. I was about twenty-six or twenty-seven at the time.

And what good was it that I read all those books in the Liberal Arts? Whether it was rhetoric, logic, geometry, music, or math, I understood it all with ease simply by reading. I had no need for a teacher. It was a gift from you, Lord my God. But I never thanked you for it.

V.

Accept this sacrificial confession which is written rather than spoken. No one tells you any secrets. A closed heart does not shut off your view.

When I was twenty-nine, a man named Faustus came to Carthage. He was a Manichean bishop and the devil used his smooth tongue as a trap. I had read and retained many philosophical works. When I compared those teachings with the verbose fables of the Manicheans I found the philosophers made the most sense. I found proof of the philosophers' theories in mathematics, the dependable orderliness of nature, and the observable evidence of the stars. I compared these things with what Manes had written so profusely and wildly on the same topics, but I could find nothing from him regarding solstices, equinoxes, or eclipses.

You have said, "The fear of the Lord, that is wisdom." (Job 28:28)

---

3. *De Pulchro et Apto*

Why, then, did Manes rush in and try to teach what he did not know? He egotistically tried to convince people that the Holy Spirit resided in him and made his ideas authoritative. His sacrilegious arrogance can be seen in the fact that he not only wrote about things of which he was ignorant, but also fabricated lies. With vain madness he tried to accredit himself as divine. We can overlook such behavior in the newly faithful, but Manes had the audacity to convince his followers that he was not an ordinary man, but the personification of your Holy Spirit.

For nearly nine years I had been looking forward to meeting Faustus. When other Manichean leaders were unable to answer my questions they always promised that when he came he would explain everything. I found him a genteel conversationalist who said the same silly things with more charm. I was thirsty. An attractive cup-bearer had brought me a lovely, but empty, cup. I had heard it all before. The ideas were not improved because they were expressed better; they did not become true because they were eloquent. Neither did I think that he was spiritually wise just because he had a handsome face and a glib tongue.

[Augustine goes on to say that he respected Faustus for admitting his ignorance on many subjects and refusing to debate that which he did not understand.]

Every desire I had to advance in this sect melted away after I met this man. He had trapped others, but without realizing it, Faustus began to untie the cords that held me.

You worked on me inwardly, Lord, and I decided to leave Carthage and teach in Rome. What persuaded me to move was not the higher pay and the greater prestige which were mentioned by my friends. The strongest reason was that I had been told that the students there behaved better. The students of Carthage are notoriously impudent and unruly. It was a simple decision. But you, "my refuge and my portion in the land of the living" (Ps. 142:5), led me to change residences for my soul's salvation.

You knew it all along, O God, but you told neither me nor my mother. She followed me, weeping and wailing, all the way to the sea-coast. She held on to me so that I would either go home with her or take her with me to Rome. I told her that I wanted to wait to see a friend off. I lied to my mother, to such a mother! That night I sneaked away. I left her behind, praying and weeping. With all those tears she asked you to prevent me from sailing. But you knew more than she did. You did, in fact, answer her prayer in its essence. You did not give her what she wanted right then, in order that you might give her what she had always been asking for. There was a good sailing wind and the shore was soon out of sight. The next morning she complained to you with frantic grief for ignoring her prayers. But, all the while, you were using my willfulness to answer her prayers, and to punish her misguided affection. She enjoyed having me with her, like most mothers, but more so. She had no idea how you would bless her, so she wept and mourned. After the shock of my departure wore off, she returned home, and I continued to Rome.

Upon arrival at Rome I became deathly ill. My mother, in ignorance of this, went right on praying for me. You are everywhere. You heard her where she was and helped me where I was.

But only my body was healed. My heart remained sacrilegious. I didn't consider myself a sinner. I assumed that some kind of strange nature sinned in me. When I did something wrong, I excused myself and accused this make-believe thing in me. My sin, therefore, was incurable.

I gathered some students together in my home and taught them rhetoric. By word of mouth I gained a reputation. But teaching had its problems in Rome also. They were more decorous, to be sure, but, as I had been warned, the students get together and switch teachers in order to evade the payment of a fee.

When I had an opportunity to apply for a position in Milan, I took it. My public speech was approved and I was chosen. It was in Milan that I met Bishop Ambrose. He was widely known as one of the world's best men, a devout and eloquent preacher. You led me to him in order that he might lead me to you. He welcomed me like a father. When I began to love him it was not because I expected to find any truth in him, but simply because he was kind to me. Little by little, I was being drawn closer to you, but I did not notice it.

I paid no particular attention to *what* Ambrose said. I only cared about *how* he said it. But after a while I began to see that Christianity could be rational. I was especially impressed with his figurative explanation of certain Old Testament passages which had killed my interest when I had taken them literally.

I decided to continue as a catechumen in the Catholic Church until I could see more clearly.

VI.

Where were you, God, during all of this? I walked in dangerous darkness and looked for you outside myself, but I did not find you. I lost all hope of ever discerning the truth.

My mother followed me across the sea, trusting you amid great peril. She even comforted the *sailors,* assuring them that they would arrive safely because you had promised her this in a vision. She found me deep in a state of spiritual struggle. I told her that while I was not yet a Christian, I was at least no longer a Manichean. This caused no display of excitement in her. She responded with quiet confidence that God would answer all of her prayers and she would see me a faithful Christian before she died. But though she was serene when talking with me, she multiplied her prayers and tears. She hurried to church regularly and devoured the things Ambrose said. She loved that man as though he were God's angel because she knew he was responsible for my present struggle. She knew I had to pass through such a crisis on my way from sickness to health.

I considered Ambrose a fortunate man by the standards of the world. He had respect of important people. Only his celibacy seemed to me to be a burden.

I wanted to ask him many questions, but his busy schedule prevented me from having a personal conversation with him. Anyone could approach him without an announcement, but when we did we would often see him reading silently and we would not want to interrupt his study. We would sit quietly and watch him at work for a while, and then go away.

But even though I never had an opportunity to pour out my soul to that holy oracle of yours, I did get to hear him every Sunday. His sermons convinced me that all those deceptive knots others had tied around the Scripture could be untied. As I listened to him, I was ashamed that I had been barking all those years, not against the Catholic faith, but against imaginary doctrines. I had impulsively spoken against things I should first have learned more about. The Church never taught the things I accused her of teaching. It was refreshing to hear Ambrose repeat so often to his congregation: "The letter killeth, but the spirit giveth life." (2 Cor. 3:6 KJV) He drew aside the veil of mystery and made clear the spiritual meaning of things which could not be accepted literally. I disagreed with nothing he said, but there were some things I still could not understand. I resisted because I did not want to fall again. I wanted to be as sure of spiritual things as that seven and three equal ten. An experience with a bad doctor engenders mistrust of even a good one.

Lord, with a gentle and merciful touch you worked on my heart. I thought of the many things I believed which I had not seen, or which happened when I was not present—so much history, so many facts about places I had never visited, so many things mentioned by others. Daily living requires belief in these things. Most of all, I was impressed with the fact that I believed I was the child of particular parents on no other authority than that I had been told it. What is so different about accepting the authority of the Bible? Since we are not able to discover the truth by reasoning, we need the Scriptures. The Bible speaks to all in clear language, and yet it also demands the close attention of scholarly minds.

I thought about these things and you were near me. I sighed and you listened. I wandered along the broad road of the world, but you did not forsake me.

I discussed such ideas with my closest friends. Alypius was from my home town. He had been one of my students. He went to Rome before I did. Incredibly, this law student developed a craving for gladiatorial games. Some fellow students took him, by friendly force and against his will, to the amphitheater on a day scheduled for those cruel and bloody contests. He told them, "You can drag my body into the place, but you can't force me to look at it or think about it. I will be with you in body, but not in spirit. I shall defeat both you and the gladiators."

When they heard this they worked even harder to drag him there. The place was already in a frenzy when they got there. He shut his eyes and tried to think of other things. Too bad he could not shut his ears! For when a gladiator went down, the crowd made a tremendous roar and he was overcome by curiosity. He opened his eyes and received a wound in his soul deeper than the one in the body of the slain man. When he saw the blood he became a savage. He did not turn away, he fixed his eyes on it and drank in the insanity with pleasure. He became one of the crowd, shouting and burning with passion.

In order that you might help him without any awareness on my part, you sent him to me. I was sitting with my students in my usual place when he came in, greeted me, and sat down with the class. I was teaching from a passage when it occurred to me that I could illustrate it with a comparison to the games. The point was both clear and amusing and it ridiculed those who are captivated by that particular madness. You know, O my God, that I was not thinking of Alypius' addiction. But the shoe fit and he wore it. Someone else may have become angry with me, but this young man was honest enough to be angry with himself. Long ago you had it written in your book: "Rebuke a wise man, and he will love thee." (Prov. 9:8)

Lord, at thirty I was still stuck in the same mire, trying to catch the things that both eluded me and hurt me. I kept saying, "I'll find it tomorrow. It will become clear and I will understand it. Things in the Church books that formerly seemed absurd no longer appear that way to me. I will climb the steps my parents started me on as a child. But where shall I look? When do I start? Ambrose is busy. I have no time for reading. Who has the books? Where can I get them? Will anyone lend them to me? I must set a special time for this. Why do I hesitate to knock? Am I afraid of what I may learn? My students only occupy my mornings; what about the rest of the day? Why don't I do this? If I did, when would I find the time to visit influential friends? When would I prepare my lessons or repair my tired mind?"

While I argued with myself in this manner my heart was blown first one way and then another by the wind. Time was passing and I put off turning to the Lord. I could not bear the thought of staying out of a woman's embrace. I never considered that you might heal this weakness because I was not familiar with you. I was tied down by this desire for deadly sweet flesh. Alypius was amazed that I, of all people, should be so preoccupied with sex. I explained that there was a great difference in his youthful experimentation, already brushed aside and forgotten, and my habitual pleasure. All it lacked was the honorable title, "marriage." Alypius decided that if it were all that important and pleasant he would get married himself just to find out what it was like. His mind, free from this bondage, marveled that I could be so enslaved.

Others urged me to get married. I asked for a girl's hand and she was promised to me. My mother had a lot to do with it. But the attractive girl was only eight years old and I had to wait until she was ten.[4]

Meanwhile my sinning got worse. The woman I slept with became

---

4. The numbers are accurate, but the original reads, "She was two years short of the age of consent, but she attracted me and I agreed to wait."

an obstacle to my marriage and had to be sent away. We had become attached to each other and this separation was very painful for me. She returned to Africa, promising me that she would never know another man, and left me our natural son. Because of my unhappiness, I was unable to return her vow. I could not bear the thought of waiting two years for my wife. In fact, I really didn't want a wife. I wanted sex. So I found another woman and actually increased the flames of my passion.

Praise be to you, glory be to you, O Fountain of Mercies! I became more wretched and you drew closer to me. You were ready to help me, but I didn't know it.

VII.

[In book seven, Augustine abruptly changes his style for a few pages. It is almost as though the psychological intensity of the preceding material made it necessary to step back for a moment into the relative safety of theology and philosophy. He discusses the nature of God and the origin of evil, and presents a convincing denunciation of astrology. He admits to a fleeting glimpse of the truth he sought and begins to recognize his need for Christ. He recalls reading the books of the Platonists with great interest, but admits that they did not go far enough and stopped short of Jesus. He tells how he turned with eagerness to the Scriptures, especially to the Pauline epistles. His former difficulties with Paul seems to evaporate and he begins to tremble with the excitement of discovery.]

VIII.

Let me remember with thanksgiving, O my God, and confess your mercies to me. Your words had taken root in my heart and you surrounded me. What I wanted now was not more certainty *about* you, but to be more certain *in* you. I was unhappy with my life. The possibilities for honor and profit no longer interested me. What still bound me was my desire for women. I had found the pearl of great price, and I should have sold everything and bought it. But I hesitated.

I went to see Simplicianus, who could be called the "spiritual father" of Ambrose. He told me of his conversations with Victorinus. Victorinus had studied Christian writings in great depth and said to Simplicianus privately, "I want you to know I am a Christian." Simplicianus answered, "I won't believe it until I see you in the church of Christ." Victorinus chuckled and said, "So it's *walls* that make Christians!" The truth of the matter was that he did not want to offend his pagan friends.

Later, after being strengthened by reading and longing, he saw that it was important to confess Jesus openly. Without any preamble, he said to Simplicianus, "Let's go to church. I want to be a Christian." It astonished Rome and filled the church with joy. The priests offered him an opportunity to make his profession of faith in private, but he preferred to do so on the platform in full view of the congregation.

He was a well-known person and his name was whispered all over the church when he stood up to speak. "Victorinus! Victorinus!" Almost as quickly as they had started that suppressed chant, they fell silent and listened. He uttered the true faith confidently, and in their love and joy, the congregation embraced him.

O God of love, we listen with special joy when we hear how the lost sheep is brought home on the happy shepherd's shoulders, or how the lost coin is recovered. The celebration in your home brings tears to our eyes when we hear how the younger son who was dead is made alive again, was lost and then found.

When your servant, Simplicianus, told me about Victorinus, I was set on fire to be like him. Simplicianus went on to tell me that the emperor Julian had made a law prohibiting Christians from teaching literature and public speaking. But Victorinus preferred to give up his school of words for your Word. This seemed to me to be both courageous and fortunate, because it gave him the opportunity to concentrate entirely on you, O Lord. I longed for such a thing. But I was bound by my own iron will.

> A perverse will produces lust.
> Lust yielded to becomes a habit.
> A habit not resisted becomes a necessity.

These were like links of a chain hanging one upon the other, and they bound me hand and foot. I had two wills: one old, one new; one carnal, one spiritual. Their conflict wasted my soul.

I was like a sleepy man unable to get up. No one wants to sleep all the time. Everyone knows it is best to be awake, but sluggishness often prevents us from shaking ourselves awake and we doze a while longer.

I knew it would be best to give myself to you and give up my lust. I had no reply when you said to me, "Awake, thou that sleepest, and arise from the dead, and Christ shall give thee light."(Eph. 5:14) You convinced me that your words were true. The only answer I could give were the groggy words: "Soon." "Right away." "In just a minute." But the words meant no particular span of time. "O wretched man that I am! who shall deliver me from the body of this death?"(Rom. 7:24)

No, O Lord, my helper and my redeemer, I will confess how you rescued me. A fellow countryman, Ponticianus, visited Alypius and me at home. He noticed a book on a table, picked it up, opened it, and was surprised to discover that it was by the Apostle Paul. He smiled and looked at me with astonishment. He was a faithful Christian, and knelt before you regularly, O God. I told him that I had studied the Scriptures very carefully.

In response, he told us about Antony, an Egyptian monk. Alypius and I listened with amazement at the things you did through him. Ponticianus went on to tell us about the large monasteries and their way of life. There was even a monastery at Milan, just outside the city, that was filled with worthy brothers under the guidance of Ambrose. We had never heard about it. He continued talking and we listened in attentive silence.

While he was speaking, you, O Lord, made me introspective in spite of myself. I saw myself and was horrified. And there was nowhere to run.

I continued trying to delay it. I prayed for chastity, adding, "but not yet!" I was afraid that you would answer my prayer too soon. I wanted my lust satisfied, not extinguished.

My conscience plagued me. "Why don't you speak? Aren't you the same man who said you couldn't throw away vanity's baggage for an uncertain truth? Then look! It is certain now, but you are still carrying the load. These people that Ponticianus is telling you about are free of their burden, and they didn't spend ten years or more debating it."

He finished his conversation and went away. I went into myself. Oh, how I condemned myself! My soul resisted. It refused to follow you, but it could find no excuse for not following. All its arguments were gone. The only thing remaining was a dreadful silence.

I turned to Alypius with a wildness in both my facial expression and my words. I cried out, "What's wrong with us? What did you hear? Common people rush into heaven while we, with all our learning, grovel around in flesh and blood!" He stared at me blankly. I did not sound like myself. My face, the tone of my voice, communicated more than my words.

The storm within me drove me out into the garden. Alypius followed me. We sat down as far from the house as we could. Greatly agitated, I knew that I had to reach a decision, that I must not go on turning and twisting like a wounded animal, this way and that, with the part of me that wanted to rise fighting the part of me that would remain earthbound.

In the agony of my indecision I tore my hair, locked my fingers together and clasped my knees. My body was obeying the slightest wish of my mind, but my mind would not obey itself. The trouble is that it really did not want it. That is why it wasn't giving a strong enough command. There were two wills, both incomplete, and what was missing in one was present in the other. It was I who willed to serve the Lord my God. It was I who was unwilling. It was I. I was at war with myself.

What held me was a trifle, but it still held me. You were in the hidden places of my soul, O Lord, and in harsh mercy increased my fear and shame in order to prevent me from giving in again and losing everything.

Inside myself I said, "Let it happen now, let it happen now." With such words I was moving toward a decision. I was almost there, but not quite. I did not return to my old ways, but I stopped to catch my breath. I attempted it again and could almost reach out and touch it, but I still didn't quite make it. The familiar evil was more powerful than the unfamiliar good. A controversy raged in my heart, myself against myself. Alypius waited by my side in silence to see the outcome of it.

But when my introspection had dredged up all of the misery of my soul and piled it up in full view of my heart, a tremendous emotional storm arose and there was a deluge of tears. In order to weep freely I got up and walked away from Alypius. I threw myself down under a fig tree and let the tears flow, a sacrifice acceptable to you. In many different words I said to you, "How long, how long? Tomorrow and tomorrow! Why not now? Why not end my uncleanness this very hour?"

And then I heard the voice of either a boy or a girl from the nearby house. It was repeating a chant, over and over, "Take up and read! Take up and read!" I immediately stopped sobbing and tried to recall if children sang those words in any game, but I could not think of any. Holding back my tears, I got up, interpreting the child's words as a command from God to open the Bible and read the first passage I should see.

I quickly returned to Alypius where I had left the Apostle's book. I snatched it up, opened it, and silently read the first thing I saw. "Let us walk honestly, as in the day; not in rioting and drunkenness, not in chambering and wantonness, not in strife and envying: But put ye on the Lord Jesus Christ, and make not provision for the flesh, to fulfil the lusts thereof." (Rom. 13:13f)

I had no desire, no need, to read further. In the instant that sentence ended, it was as if a peaceful light shone in my heart and all the darkness of doubt vanished.

Marking the place, I closed the book and calmly told Alypius everything. He surprised me by telling me that he had been having a similar struggle and asked to see what I had read. When I showed him he read on to the next line, "Gladly receive one who is weak in the faith . . ."* (Rom. 14:1) He told me that he applied this to himself. Without any troubled hesitation, he joined me.

We went to my mother and told her what had happened. She was overcome with joyful exultation and praised you. She saw that you had given her more than she had asked. You had converted me to yourself. I no longer sought a wife or this world's prizes. You changed her mourning into joy, far greater joy than she had ever dreamed of, a joy deeper and purer than she would ever find in grandchildren of my flesh.

IX.

Where was my freedom of choice all those years? From what dark cavern did you call it forth when I bowed my head and you, Christ Jesus, placed your easy yoke and light burden on my shoulders? What a joy it was to renounce the joys I was afraid to lose! You threw them out of me and took their place.

The day arrived when I gave up teaching rhetoric. You freed my tongue as you had freed my heart. With my friends, I vacationed in the country.

When I read the Psalms of David, those spiritual songs, I cried to you. I was only a beginner resting for a while in the country with another catechumen, Alypius, but I was set on fire by the Psalms and wanted to sing them to the whole world. I wish the Manichees could have seen me when I read Psalm 4, and been able to perceive what was going on inside me.

> "Hear me when I call, O God of my righteousness.
> You helped me when I was in distress,
> Have mercy upon me, and hear my prayer."* (Ps. 4:1)

Even if they had seen and heard me, they could not have understood that I was closely in your presence.

I wrote your bishop, Ambrose. I told him of my evil past and my present desire. I asked him to recommend a book of the Bible which could help me get started. He suggested Isaiah. But I did not understand the first part of that prophet's book, and imagining that it would all be the same, I put it aside. I thought I could return to it later when I was more familiar with the Lord's language.

The holiday over, we left the country and returned to Milan for baptism. Alypius also wanted to be born again in you. He possessed the necessary humility. He had enough control of his body to walk the frozen soil of Italy in his bare feet. The boy Adeotatus, conceived by my flesh in sin, also accompanied us. You had made him well. He was unusually bright for a boy less than fifteen. His intelligence was your gift, O Lord, my God. The only thing I contributed to him was the sin.

Together, we were baptized,⁵ and all anxiety regarding the past departed. I could not meditate enough upon the depth of your plan for our salvation. The singing in church made me weep.

You, Lord, sent Evodius to us from our home town. We considered where we might serve you best and decided to return to Africa. When we got to Ostia on the Tiber, my mother fainted. She quickly regained consciousness and asked, "Where was I?" Noting our concern, she said, "This is where you will bury your mother." My Christian brother told her he wished she could die at home and not in a foreign land. She did

---

5. Easter, 387.

not approve of his concern for earthly things and said to me, "Listen to that!" Then she addressed both of us. "Bury this body anywhere. Don't concern yourselves about it. I ask only one thing of you, that you remember me at the altar of the Lord, wherever you are." She was too ill to talk much more then, but later she talked to some of my friends in my absence. She told them, "Nothing is far from God. I have no fear that he will not know where to find me and raise me up at the end of the world."

On the ninth day of her illness—she was fifty-six and I was thirty-three—her devout and holy soul was freed from her body.

Evodius took up the psalter and started singing a Psalm. The household responded with singing. Many other devout people heard us and gathered there. Preparations began for burial while I conversed with those who thought I should not be left alone.

After the funeral, I fell asleep. I felt much better when I woke up. I recited some verses of Ambrose in the privacy of my bedroom.[6] And since only you could hear me, I let my tears flow.

Lord, I confess it in writing. Anyone can read and interpret it for himself. If he finds it sinful, let him not look on me with contempt. I wept for my mother for a small part of an hour, for she was dead who had wept for me that I should live in your sight.

I believe you have already done what I am asking now, O Lord. Let her rest in peace, together with her only husband, whom she also won to you. And inspire, O my Lord and God, all who read these words to remember at your altar your servant, Monica, with Patricius, her husband, by whose bodies you gave me life in some way I don't understand. Then, even more than through my own prayers, the thing my mother asked of me at the end of her life will be given through the prayers of many because I wrote these confessions.

---

6. Deus creator omnium   God, creator of all,
    polique rector vestiens   Director of the heavens,
    diem decoro lumine,   You clothe the day with light,
    noctem sopora gratia,   The night with pleasant sleep,

    artus solutos ut quies   That rest may weary limbs
    reddat laboris usui   Restore for more labor,
    mentesque fessas allevet   Lighten our weary minds,
    luctusque solvat anxios.   And untie our anxious sorrow.

X.–XIII.

[The remaining four books of the *Confession* attempt to present "not what I used to be, but what I am now, while writing my confessions. Many want to know, from my own words, what I am inside myself." And so the style of the book changes from primarily a confession of sin to a confession of faith. There is a penetrating study of the nature of memory, time, eternity and creation. His analysis of the opening chapters of Genesis makes rewarding reading. An example of this closing section is taken from book XII in which Augustine seriously ponders what he would have done if he had been Moses and the Lord God had asked him to write the book of Genesis.]

When one man contends, "Moses meant what I say," and another disagrees, "No, he meant what I say," it seems to me that it is nearer the truth to say, "Why can't he have meant both, if both of you are correct? And if someone would see a third or a fourth or any number of meanings in the same language, why can't we believe that Moses meant them all?" God has adapted the Bible to many interpretations.

Without a doubt—and I do not hesitate to speak from my heart—if I had to write with such great authority I would attempt to write in such a way that my words would communicate as much trust as possible to each reader, rather than to write down one true meaning so obvious that it would prohibit any other meaning even though there was nothing offensive in the alternate interpretations.

BERNARD OF CLAIRVAUX:
TREATISE ON LOVING GOD
SERMONS ON THE SONG OF SONGS

Bernard of Clairvaux was born in 1090 near Dijon, France. He was uncomfortable with the secular world and persuaded twenty-nine friends and relatives to go with him to the monastery at Cîteaux. By 1115 he was sent out as an abbot to establish a new Cistercian house at Clairvaux, an isolated, sparsely inhabited valley. In this remote location up to seven hundred monks joined Bernard in a quiet life of agriculture and contemplation. He taught a strict asceticism. He enjoyed fasting so much it was necessary at least once for his superiors to order him to eat. For thirty-eight years he lived in a small cell that contained only a straw mattress. His chair was an irregularity in the wall.

There is little doubt that Bernard of Clairvaux was one of the most influential individuals of his day. His involvement in politics and reform produced outstanding achievements. He became the leading representative and debater for Pope Innocent II. He traveled widely, and until his death in 1153 his advice was received by the highest authorities.

St. Bernard was trained in the classics, and while he quoted classical authors but rarely, his style of writing shows their influence. There is a liquidity in his Latin that is lost in any translation. Here is an easy specimen: "... *se solum decipit, quem solum excipit* ..." His prose reads like poetry. On the last page of the edition of his *Sermons on the Song of Songs* listed in the bibliography you will find a unique quotation arranged in lines that draw attention to his metrical style.

The Treatise, *On Loving God,* is a brief tract expressing the spirituality of the Church. A few personal glimpses shine through in spite of his denials of any interest in speaking about himself. The piece contains no date, but it was addressed to "the illustrious Lord Haimeric, Cardinal-Deacon and Chancellor of the See of Rome," and we know that Haimeric died in 1141.

The Treatise, taken together with his *Sermones in Cantica Canticorum,* provides us with a clear view of Bernard of Clairvaux's spirituality. Unfortunately, his sermons are long and rambling. Only the dedicated student is likely to read them. In this rendering you will be exposed to a sprinkling of his best moments. The power of these passages is so great they are likely to find their way into many modern sermons and homilies, even in the inadequate form in which they are printed here.

As an aside, let it be pointed out that any professor of Old Testament Exegesis today would not be inclined to give St. Bernard high grades for his work on *The Song of Songs.* But somehow, it doesn't seem to matter that he interprets this unique book the way he does.[1] Call his text a pretext if you will, his message is so vital we are immediately with him, and we stay with him to the end.

TREATISE ON LOVING GOD
I.

You have asked me to tell you why and how God is to be loved. God himself is the reason why; without limit[2] is how. For the wise, that is answer enough. But now I will speak more elaborately, if less profoundly, for the benefit of those whose minds are less agile.

There are two reasons for loving God: no one is more worthy of your love, and no one can return more in response to our love.

God deserves our love because he first loved us. His love for us was genuine because he sought nothing for himself. Notice whom he loves. "We were enemies of God, but he turned us into his friends through the death of his Son."* (Rom. 5:10) Therefore, God's love was unconditional. How much did he love? The answer is in St. John: "For God so loved the world, that he gave his only begotten Son . . ." (John 3:16) The Son, speaking of himself, said: "Greater love hath no man than this, that a man lay down his life for his friends." (John 15:13) The wicked, then, should love the Righteous One in return.

---

1. See the General Introduction for more on this problem.
2. Latin, *sine modo.*

II.

Secular persons may not acknowledge that God ought to be loved. But even they are hard-pressed to ignore his goodness to them. Who provided them with food, eyesight, and air? It would be ridiculous to try to make a list of God's gifts to them. The very dignity which sets us apart from the beasts is a gift to us from him. The same is true of our rational minds and moral virtue. We are made what we are by a power not our own. It is a gift. The Apostle cautions: "If God is the source of all you have, how can you brag about it? It is a gift!"* (1 Cor. 4:7) So then, as the Scripture says, "If you must boast, boast in the Lord."* (1 Cor. 1:31)

While we should be cautious of holding too low an opinion of ourselves, we should be even more afraid of thinking we are better than we are. It is dangerous to presume that any good in us is the result of our own efforts. We become arrogant. Not only do we fail to give God that credit due him; we actually despise him.

Everyone, believer and unbeliever alike, has a responsibility to respond to God's providential care with total love. That this is not ordinarily the case is affirmed by the Scripture. "All seek their own, not the things which are Jesus Christ's." (Phil. 2:21) ". . . for the imagination of man's heart is evil from his youth." (Gen. 8:21)

III.

It is the faithful who understand how fully they need Jesus and his death on the cross. Seeing his love, they desire to return what little they can. Those who know they are loved are better able to love. The one who is forgiven more loves more. Seeing the wounds of Christ, the faithful says, ". . . Comfort me with apples, for I am sick with love."* (Song 2:5)

IV.

Who is it that remembers God? It certainly is not "a stubborn and rebellious generation" (Ps. 78:8) to whom Christ says, "But woe unto you that are rich! for ye have received your consolation." (Luke 6:24)

Instead, it is those who can say, "I remember God, and was troubled: I complained, and my spirit made diligent search." (Ps. 77:3) Our soul, Christ's bride, loves ardently. But even when she thinks she is completely in love she feels that her love is inadequate because she is loved so much. And that is true. How could she love as much in return? God loves with all his being, the complete Trinity loves, if "complete" is not a misnomer for the infinite and incomprehensible.

V. & VI.

[These sections hammer away repeatedly at the assertion that God is worthy of our love. There are thirty-five quotations from, or allusions to, Scripture. The entire work contains more than three hundred biblical references. They pour from Bernard of Clairvaux like water from a fountain.]

VII.

Now let's see how it can help us to love him. While we should not have any ulterior motives for loving God, rewards will come. They are not the results of bargaining or legal transactions. Love is spontaneous. The only reward love seeks is someone to love. If you are looking for something else, it isn't love. Moreover, it is the unwilling, not the willing, that we have to ply with favors. Who would ever think of rewarding a person for enjoying himself? You don't have to bribe a hungry man to eat, or a mother to nurse her child. The soul that loves God expects nothing in return. If it did, then it would love that prize instead of God.

God alone can satisfy our desires. A man with a lovely wife will look lustfully at a more attractive woman. A well-dressed person wants more expensive clothes. A rich man envies anyone richer than himself. You can find men who already own farms and have great possessions, still striving, day in and day out, to add another field to their estates. They remodel homes already fit for kings. See their restless ambition for promotion and honors. The reason why there is never any relaxing end to all of this gathering and climbing is because none of these objects can be considered the highest or the best. It is not very intelligent to desire what can never satisfy. While enjoying wealth, you keep searching for something you still lack. You run back and forth from one pleasure to another, getting tired, but never satisfied. Who can own everything? Whatever you cling to, you are surely going to lose one day. You are running down a twisting road and you will die before you reach the end of it.

Eventually, we will come to say

"Whom have I in heaven but thee
and there is none upon earth that I desire besides thee." (Ps. 73:25)

Anything else is doomed to failure. Life is too short, strength too limited, competition too fierce. The long road wears us out.

VIII.
THE FIRST STEP IN LOVE: LOVE OF SELF AND NEIGHBOR

Love is natural. It is not the result of teaching an idea. It is part of our being. To keep our love from becoming self-centered, we are given this commandment: "Love thy neighbor as thyself." (Matt. 22:39) Those who share our nature should benefit from shared love. Personal restraint is necessary. The person who indulges himself needs to remember that his neighbor has identical privileges. Temperance is the safeguard. Don't serve the enemy of your soul with nature's gifts; serve your neighbor. God will give you the means to do it. It is written: "But seek ye first the kingdom of God, and his righteousness; and all these things shall be added unto you; (Matt. 6:33)

But it is not possible to love your neighbor unless you love God. If you love God first, then you can love your neighbor in God.

IX.
THE SECOND STEP IN LOVE:
LOVE OF GOD FOR PERSONAL REASONS

It is advantageous to love God. Some things we cannot do for ourselves. We need divine help. If we are faced with many difficulties we will turn to God for help with increasing frequency. And as God continues to help, even the coldest heart will be warmed. The experience of his freeing grace will lead us to the next step.

THE THIRD STEP IN LOVE:
LOVING GOD BECAUSE HE IS GOD

Our human weakness and dependence upon God will result in an intimacy with him. "O taste and see that the Lord is good . . ." (Ps. 34:8) Personal familiarity with God's goodness is a better incentive to pure love of him than all of our troubles together. This expressed by the Samaritans to the woman at the well: "Now we believe, not because of thy saying: for we have heard him ourselves, and know that this is indeed the Christ, the Savior of the world." (John 4:42) We become like them when we say to our body, "We love God now, not because of your needs, but because we have found out for ourselves how good the Lord is." If we feel this way we will have little difficulty loving our neighbor. If we really love God, we will love what belongs to God. We love in the same manner as we have been loved. We care about others even as Christ cared. We love the Lord not because he is good to us, but because the Lord is good. And now we love God as God, and not for any personal favors.

X.
THE FOURTH STEP IN LOVE:
ACCEPTANCE OF SELF IN GOD

We will find happiness when we no longer love ourselves except for God. When will flesh and blood, this clay pot, this earthly house, understand that? When will this new affection be felt, this divine intoxication, this forgetting of self, this perception of brokenness that rushes toward God, clings to him, becomes united with him in Spirit? When that happens we can say, "My flesh and my heart faileth: but God is the strength of my heart, and my portion for ever." (Ps. 73:26) Anyone who tastes something as rare as this, even if only for once in a lifetime, and that but for a second, will be blessed. To lose yourself, as though you did not exist, to become nothing, is not a human emotion. It is a divine experience. When it happens, the sinful world will envy you, evil will disturb you, the body will become a burden, and concern for others will call you back with a jolt. The return will be mandatory. You must make the violent transition to your ordinary existence, and you will cry, "O wretched man that I am! who shall deliver me from the body of this death?" (Rom. 7:24).

Now our personal cares and needs will no longer take first place. We will want God's will to be done in us. We will pray every day, "Thy will be done on earth as it is in heaven." (Matt. 6:10) O pure and sacred love! It frees us from personal vanity. It is cleansing to go through such an experience. It is like a drop of water disappearing in a cask of wine. The water begins to look and to taste like wine. It is like iron melting in a fire, like air infused with sunshine. Our human feelings dissolve mysteriously and flow into God's will. Nothing human remains.

This is not likely to happen until we have been faithful to the commandment: "Love the Lord thy God with all thy heart, and with all thy soul, and with all thy mind, and with all thy strength." (Mark 12:30) It will not happen until the heart is not distracted by the body, and the soul is free. The fourth degree of love is experienced as a spiritual body. And it is not won by our efforts. It is a gift from God. We will arrive at this highest love when we are no longer enslaved by any physical desire or upset by any difficulty and are eagerly seeking the Lord's joy.

XI.

Those souls which are free of their bodies are completely absorbed into that great ocean of eternal light. But even after such an experience, there remains, until death, an incompleteness. We are naturally attached to our bodies.

[Bernard goes on to speak of how the flesh can be a helpful companion for a good spirit. He then tacks on a letter he had written earlier on this subject, explaining, "It is easier to copy what I have already dictated than to write something new." In essence, the letter affirms that God is love, and that love begets love.]

SERMONS ON THE SONG OF SONGS

I will speak to you differently than I would address secular people. This will not be milk for spiritual infants, but solid food for the mature. Prepare your mouth for chewing the delicious bread from *The Song of Songs*. The Lord himself shall be known in the breaking of this bread. I am not able to do it. With you, I look for meat from God.

We look to you, O Lord. Your children seek bread. In mercy, break your bread with my hands.

It is significant that this scripture was given the title, *The Song of Songs*. It is not just, *A Song*. The Bible contains many songs, but this one is different from all the others. There are songs of thanksgiving for deliverance, songs of mothers and prophets. But King Solomon was inspired to sing the praises of Christ and his Church, to write a song about holy love, the mysteries of the eternal marriage, an anthem expressing the soul's desires. It is a wedding song in figures of speech. Its melody is not heard by all, but only by the Bridegroom and the Bride, the singer and the One sung about.

"Let him kiss me with the kisses of his mouth . . ." (1:2 KJV).

I see in this verse the longing of the Fathers for the advent of Christ. They are weary now of Moses' stammering speech, Isaiah's unclean lips, Jeremiah's youthfulness. They want the One to whom they point to speak for himself. Let *his* lips cover me with kisses.

Today, we can read from the book of experience. Not everyone can say, "Let him kiss me with the kisses of his mouth," but whoever has been spiritually kissed by Christ will always desire it again. Of course, a sinful soul like mine cannot claim any such grace.

This is what I advise: don't try to lift yourself to the Divine Bridegroom's mouth, but lie with me at the Lord's feet. Let's be afraid to look up to heaven for fear of being blinded by the light.

"Let him kiss me with the kisses of his mouth." Who is it that speaks? It is the Bride, the soul thirsting for God. Think of this as compared with other relationships. A slave fears his lord, a laborer looks for his paycheck, a student listens to his teacher, a son honors his father. But she who seeks a kiss loves. Love is the highest natural gift, and it is highest of all when it is returned to its source—God. The bride and bridegroom share everything, They have one inheritance, one home, one table, one couch. In fact, they are one flesh.

". . . Thy name is an ointment poured fourth, therefore do the virgins love thee." (1:3 KJV)

The Holy Spirit works in us and through us. We receive and we give. This verse deals with the gifts of God we are to pass on to others. "Thy name is an ointment poured forth." We must be careful not to give to someone else what was intended for ourselves. We must also be sure that we do not keep that which was given us to be passed on to others. In other words, you will lose what is yours if you start giving it away before your soul is half-filled, but you are obligated to pass on what is surplus.

Think of yourself as a container rather than a pipe. A pipe pours a liquid out as fast as it takes it in. A container waits until it is filled before it overflows. It gives away without any loss to itself. The Church needs more containers these days. It already has plenty of pipes. They are ready to teach what they don't understand, and to be authorities without learning the rules.

If I have a little oil, like the widow Elijah met, should I give it to you? No! I will keep it for my own anointing unless the prophet orders me to do otherwise. If you desire and insist that I have more than I think I do, I reply, "Go and get some for yourself." When you are full, then [with reserve and discretion] you may pour out of your fullness. I have no desire to be helped at your expense. If it hurts you, how can it do me any good? Help me, if you can, with your overflow. If you can't, spare yourself.

"If thou know not, O thou fairest among women, go thy way forth by the footsteps of the flock, and feed thy kids beside the shepherd's tents." (1:8 KJV)

Moses once boldly prayed, "Show me thy glory" (Ex. 33:18 KJV). He had already found favor with God. The vision he received was nowhere near what he asked for, but it helped him toward what he sought. It is the same way with the Bride. She asks for a great favor and is rebuked. But this is for her benefit. Humility is a necessary prerequisite for grace. When you are humiliated, grace is certainly on the way. But it is not humiliation that justifies us and brings us righteousness. It is humility. Some people are humiliated without responding with humility. They resent the humiliation instead of bearing it patiently, willingly. Those who resent it are guilty. Those who are patient are innocent. Those who bear it willingly are righteous. Yes, innocence is a part of righteousness, but it is only the one who can see the value of being humbled that is completely righteous. Anyone who is unwillingly humiliated, or who complains about it, can't understand that. The humble person has changed humiliation into humility.

If you want an example, consider Paul. "Most gladly therefore will I rather glory in my infirmities, that the power of Christ may rest upon me." (2 Cor. 12:9) He doesn't say he bears his weakness patiently, but that he willingly revels in it. There is no sadness in it. Other people will criticize you and hurt you, but they can't make you humble. Only you can decide to gladly suffer silently for God's sake.

"If thou know not . . . go thy way forth . . ." It is as if he had said, "You are not worthy of this contemplation of heavenly things. Leave me and return to worldly pleasures." The soul, then, should not be too eager to reach for heavenly things while still earthbound. It may be overwhelmed by glory. It may receive more than it can bear.

"A bundle of myrrh is my well-beloved unto me; he shall lie all night betwixt my breasts. My beloved is unto me as a cluster of camphire in the vineyards of Engedi." (1:13f)

He has been called "King," but now he is "well-beloved." The title of respect has been exchanged for a term of endearment. The one who was distant is not quite near. The "bundle of myrrh," in its bitterness, represents the suffering the Bride will have to endure for the Beloved's sake. If you are wise, you will keep that bouquet of myrrh in your bosom at all times. You will be glad to share his bitter sufferings.

Since my conversion I have always gathered this little bouquet of myrrh from among my Lord's persecution and suffering. I keep it in my heart to make up for the many qualities I lack. I pick them from his difficulties as an infant, his effort in preaching, his travel fatigue, his prayers in the night, his temptations when he fasted, his sympathetic tears, the tricks of those who tried to catch him in the things he said, the dangers he faced among hypocrites, the insults, the spitting, the scourging, the nails that pierced his flesh, and all the other indignities he accepted for our salvation. Like walking through the woods, I wander among these things and pluck here and there a stem for my bouquet of myrrh.

This little bouquet is precious to me. I will never let it go. I will keep it between my breasts. There is wisdom in meditating on these things. When I face adversity, they give me strength. When everything is going well, they keep my perspective in balance. You know how often I talk about these things. God knows they are continually in my heart. My philosophy is to know "Christ, and him crucified." (1 Cor. 2:2 KJV) There is no higher philosophy. I don't need to ask him where he rests, because he dwells in my heart. Neither do I have to inquire about the location of his flock, the way the Bride does, because I see my Savior on the cross.

You should do the same. Gather a bouquet of myrrh and protect it in your heart. Don't carry it on your shoulder where you can't see it. Carry it in front of you. If you can smell its fragrance, it will never be a burden.

And if the Beloved is in the myrrh, he will also be in the sweetness of the grape. My Lord Jesus is myrrh to me in his death, but he is grapes to me in his resurrection. He died for our sins and rose for our justification. Now we can be dead to sin and alive to righteousness. If you have mourned because of your sin, you have tasted bitter myrrh. If you desire to live a holier life, you have traded that bitterness for the "wine that maketh glad the heart of man." (Ps. 104:15 KJV) Then you may honestly say, "My beloved is unto me as a cluster of camphire in the vineyards of Engedi."

"My beloved is like a rose or a young hart: behold, he standeth behind our wall, he looketh forth at the windows, showing himself through the lattice." (2:9 KJV)

These words literally describe the Bridegroom as having quickly approached the Bride's house, and now stands outside, modestly hesitating to enter. The spiritual meaning, however, requires another interpretation. The "wall" is our flesh. The nearness of the Bridegroom is the incarnation of the Word. The "lattice" and "windows," it seems to me, are the five senses and our emotions, by means of which he experienced human needs. "Surely he hath borne our griefs, and carried our sorrows . . ." (Isa. 53:4 KJV) He always knew about these things, but now he has a concrete experience of them. And while "the mercy of the Lord is from everlasting" (Ps. 103:17 KJV), that experience taught him a new dimension of mercy. This is what is meant by the statement, "(He) was in all points tempted like as we are, yet without sin . . . that we may obtain mercy . . ." (Heb. 4:15f KJV) In other words, he became what he already was and learned what he already knew. He wanted his own windows and lattices in order to know what it's like to live this life.

Let me explain what it means when it says the Bridegroom is near enough to look through the lattices of our windows. God is equally present everywhere, but, by his grace, some people are more aware of his nearness than others. Only a few can say, as the Bride says, that only one wall stands between them.

Who has not succumbed to sin? Each time we sin, we erect another wall between ourselves and God. Our windows and lattices are our confessions of sin. We open our soul to the depth of his gaze. When I confess my sins I open the narrow lattice. When my heart is warmed by love as I consider God's goodness and mercy and I break into songs of praise to him, then I open a much larger window, and the Bridegroom looks in with quickened interest.

"[Re]turn, my beloved, and be thou like a roe or a young hart upon the mountains of Bether." (2:17 KJV)

The soul that loves God is his Bride. I will speak of my personal experience with the Bridegroom. It may not sound like much when you hear it, but I won't mind that. A spiritual person will not object, and one who is not spiritual simply won't understand a thing I say.

I speak foolishly. But I cannot but admit that the Word has often come even to me. I have never noticed the precise moment when he arrived. I feel his presence and then I remember that he was with me. Sometimes I have a premonition that he is coming to me. But I have never been able to put my finger on the exact instant when he arrived or departed. What path he uses to enter or leave my soul is a mystery to me. "His footsteps are not known" (Ps. 77:19 KJV), as it is written.

He could not enter through my eyes, because he has no color. Neither could it be through my ears, since he makes no sound. It was not my nose that detected his presence, because his sweetness blends with the mind, not the air. It could not have been my tongue that noticed him, for one does not eat or drink him. And the sense of touch is of no value for discerning a presence that is not physical. How did he enter my soul?

Perhaps he did not enter at all. Maybe he was never outside. But how can I say that he exists within me when I know that there is nothing good in me? When I am at my best, the Word still towers high above me. Because I wanted to know, I searched the lowest depths of my being, but he was deeper still. the Apostle was right, "In him we live and move and have our being." (Acts 17:28) Blessed is that person in whom he dwells, who lives for him and is motivated by him.

How, then, did I know he was in me? I couldn't miss it! It affected me in an undeniable way. My heart was softened and my soul roused from its slumber. He went to work in me. He cleared and cultivated the soil of my soul. He planted and watered and brought light to dark places. He opened what was closed, and warmed what was cold. He made the crooked "straight, and the rough places plain" (Isa. 40:4), and I sang, "Bless the Lord, O my soul: and all that is within me, bless his holy name." (Ps. 103:1)

Though my senses felt nothing, I knew the Bridegroom was present by the movement of my heart. I saw his power at work in me. He destroyed my desire to sin; he controlled my responses. He showed me my "secret sins in the light of (his) countenance." (Ps. 90:8 KJV) I am familiar with his gentle kindness through first-hand experience. The small improvements I have been able to make, the renewal of my mind and spirit—these things convince me of his love. I have seen a fraction of his glory and it was awesome.

When the Word decides to depart from me, it is like fire being taken from under a boiling kettle. My excited devotion diminishes. That is my clue that he is gone. And then I am always sorrowful and eagerly wait for his next return. Having experienced the joy of his indwelling once, I, like the Bride, cry out, "Return!" I will pray that prayer as long as I live. As many times as he leaves me I will always call him back. And I will pray that when he returns he will not come with empty hands, but "full of grace and truth" (John 1:14 KJV), the way he ordinarily does, the way he did yesterday and the day before.

It is in this way that I can compare him with "a roe or a young hart." Grace is as happy as a fawn, and truth is as clear as the roe's sharp eyesight. With both grace and truth together, I don't feel as though I need to hide anything. Truth doesn't allow any secrets, and grace makes secrets unnecessary. John wrote ". . . grace and truth came by Jesus Christ." (John 1:17) And if the Lord, the Word, the Bridegroom of the soul, comes to me with only one of these, he is no longer the Bridegroom, but a judge. May I never experience him as judgmental! Serious, yes. Let his penetrating gaze reveal my true self and produce humility. But, at the same time, let him come into me as a prancing deer, leaping over my sins in mercy. May he enter as "upon the mountains of Bether," joyous and radiant, sent to me by the Father who is kind and gentle. He will actually become the Bridegroom of the soul that is looking for him.

[St. Bernard died before he had finished preaching through *The Song of Songs*. His last sermon carried the series through chapter three, verse four. In it, he explains how the soul and the Word have enough in common for union to be an easy, natural thing, and how God is looking for us long before we begin our search for him.]

UGOLINO: THE LITTLE FLOWERS OF ST.
FRANCIS (ACTUS-FIORETTI)
FRANCIS OF ASSISI: WRITINGS

T o fully appreciate the writings of Francis of Assisi, it is necessary to be familiar with the man. A good biography of St. Francis is required reading. For newcomers, the brief sketch by G.K. Chesterton has much to commend it.

This little man of God comes down to us across seven centuries trailing clouds of glory, the individual particles of which are difficult to sort out. Modern Franciscan research has uncovered and catalogued a vast collection of material related to this remarkable individual. The present sample presents a few selections from the famous *Fioretti* which were collected about a hundred years after the saint's death. While much of this material is clearly of a legendary nature, these vignettes give us penetrating insights into the character and personality of Francis as perceived by those who knew him. Ugolino di Monte Santa Maria gathered this largely oral tradition in a Latin volume he entitled *The Acts of St. Francis and His Companions (Actus Beati Francisci et Sociorum Ejus).* It soon appeared in a slightly shorter Italian edition known as *The Little Flowers of St. Francis (I Fioretti di San Francesco).* It became an exceptionally popular book. Of all the selections in this anthology, this one was the most difficult to represent completely. The rewritten passages merely hint at the whole.

Following the selections from the *Fioretti* are some writings of Francis of Assisi himself. He did not leave us great quantities of written material, but each piece we have is a sparkling gem of spirituality. For example, one of his most famous writings is a little blessing he gave his close friend, Leo. It contains just five words: *Dominus bene dicat Leo te.* But note the originality of the placement of Leo's name between the verb and the object. "The Lord bless—Leo—you!" This created a very special, individualized blessing which Brother Leo is reported to have carried next to his heart for the remainder of his life. Leo, incidentally, was Francis' secretary who often wrote as the saint dictated.

All of Francis of Assisi's writings are in Latin with the exception of the beautiful "Song of Our Brother Sun." He wrote this canticle near the end of his life in his native tongue, Italian.

A few essential facts of his life (1182–1226) will enhance your appreciation of the selections that follow. Francis grew up among the lovely hills of central Italy, the son of a prosperous merchant. He was a handsome, gregarious, generous, friendly socialite who enjoyed being something of a troubadour. After severe disappointment and a misunderstanding with his father, he made a dramatic declaration of independence and faith. It is recorded that he stripped himself of all clothing, laid all his earthly possessions on the floor, and said, "Until now I have called Pietro Bernadone my father, but now I desire to serve God. I return to him money, clothing, everything." Francis then began a life of absolute self-denial and poverty. He organized the Brothers Minor (*Fratres minores*) which eventually became the Franciscan Order.

As the years went by, Francis turned to a life of solitary contemplation and prayer and was drawn into a depth of spirituality far beyond common experience. He died at the age of forty-five.

UGOLINO: *ACTUS-FIORETTI*
HOW TO FIND PERFECT JOY

St. Francis and Brother Leo were walking from Perugia to St. Mary of the Angels. It was winter and they were suffering from the cold. St. Francis said, "Brother Leo, even if all the Friars Minor lived a life of exemplary holiness and integrity, make a note that perfect joy is not in that."

They walked further and St. Francis spoke again. "Brother Leo, even if a Friar Minor restores sight to the blind, drives out demons, grants hearing to the deaf, heals the crippled, gives speech to the dumb and raises the dead, write it down that perfect joy is not in that."

And after walking a little further, he again spoke out strongly. "Brother Leo, if a Friar Minor understood all languages and knew everything about science and the Bible, if he had the gift of prophecy, write this down and underline it: perfect joy is not in that.''

And continuing on their way, St. Francis added, ''Brother Leo, even if a Friar Minor were able to preach well enough to convert every infidel to Christ, put it on paper that perfect joy is not there.''

After about two miles of this, Brother Leo asked him to please tell him where perfect joy *could* be found.

And this is what he said: ''If, when we get to St. Mary of the Angels, cold and wet and hungry, and the attendant comes to answer our ringing at the gate, and he is angry and asks us who we are, and we answer that we are two brothers, and he doesn't believe us, and sends us away because he thinks we are thieves and robbers, and we have to stay out in the snow and rain without any food until dark; then, if we are able to endure such treatment patiently, without getting upset and without complaining, and if we will concede that he is probably correct in his judgment of us, then, Brother Leo, write it down that perfect joy is there!

''The greatest gift which Christ can give us is the ability to conquer ourselves so that we can accept suffering, insults, and humiliation for his sake. The Apostle Paul says, 'God forbid that I should glory, save in the cross of our Lord Jesus Christ . . .' '' (Gal. 6:14 KJV)

GOD SPEAKS THROUGH BROTHER LEO

In the early days of the Order, St. Francis was with Brother Leo in an isolated place where they could find no breviary for their morning prayers. St. Francis instructed Brother Leo to respond to his extemporaneous prayers by repeating and affirming what he heard. Leo agreed to do so and told Francis to begin.

The saint then said to himself, ''Brother Francis, you are guilty of much sin and ought to go to hell.''

And Leo answered, ''God will do so many good things through you that you will go to heaven.''

''Don't say that, Brother Leo! I told you to repeat what I said.''

Leo agreed that he would do so the next time.

Beating his breast and crying and sighing, St. Francis prayed, "Oh Lord God, I have sinned against you and deserve to be damned!"

And Brother Leo answered, "Oh Brother Francis, God will distinguish you among the blessed!"

At this, Francis spoke impatiently to Leo, commanding him under the rule of holy obedience to respond in a proper manner. "Then you, Brother Leo, Little Lamb, say, 'Surely you are not worthy of God's mercy!' "

Assured that Leo would speak as he was told, St. Francis knelt and raised his hands toward heaven. He said, "Francis, you are a wicked sinner. How can God have mercy on anyone as bad as you?"

When Brother Leo responded, he said, "God's mercy is infinitely greater than your sins. He will be merciful to you and bless you."

This created a gentle wonder in St. Francis and he asked Leo, "Brother, why do you break the rule of obedience?"

With much humility and reverence Leo replied, "God knows I have tried to answer as you want, but God makes me say what he likes and not what I like."

St. Francis was astonished and said, "Brother, please answer me this time the way I instructed you." And with tears he repeated his previous prayer.

Again, Leo could not control himself and replied, "But God will have mercy on you and fill you with his grace. He will exalt you because whoever humbles himself shall be exalted, and that's all I can say because God is speaking through my lips!"

And they kept up this beautiful contest all night.

TWO SAINTS DINE TOGETHER

St. Clare, with one of her sisters as a companion, left her cloister at San Damiano and visited St. Francis at St. Mary of the Angels. He had prepared a table upon the bare earth in his usual manner and a group of brothers and sisters sat down to eat. St. Francis spoke about God with such sincerity and devotion that everyone in the room was infused with the grace of God. They were enraptured.

From a distance, it appeared to the citizens of Assisi and Bettona that the forest was on fire. They ran to the scene prepared to combat a terrible blaze. But when they got to St. Mary of the Angels they could find no fire. All they saw was St. Francis and St. Clare and their friends sitting around a meager table, contemplating God. They understood that it had been a heavenly fire which they had seen and they left in awe and wonder.

A SERMON FOR THE BIRDS

While walking near Cannara and Bevegna, St. Francis saw an unusual flocking of various birds in the trees along the road. It was such an impressive gathering of birds he told his companions to wait for him on the road while he went into the field to speak to "our sisters, the birds."

When he began to preach, the birds came closer to him exhibiting no sign of fear. Brother James of Massa, a trustworthy man of God, said that he heard this from Brother Masseo, who was there.

In essence, this is what St. Francis said to the birds: "My little sisters, remember to praise God because you are indebted to him. You are free to fly wherever you please. He has given you beautiful clothes. He provides you with food and teaches you how to sing. He saved you with Noah's ark and helped you to be fruitful and multiply. Thank him for the air you fly in. Thank him for the water you drink from rivers and springs. Thank him for the high cliffs and trees where you can build your nests. Thank him that you are not required to sow or reap, spin or weave. God gives you and your children everything you need. Such things can only mean that God loves you very much. Therefore, my little sisters, remember to thank and praise God."

The birds responded visibly to his preaching. When he dismissed them with the sign of the cross they flew into the air singing a lovely song.

THE WOLF OF GUBBIO

The town of Gubbio was scourged by the presence of an extremely fierce and aggressive wolf. The people were terrified of it and hesitated to go out of the city gate.

When St. Francis visited Gubbio he was warned to stay inside for his own safety. But instead of being afraid, he went looking for the wolf. A few peasants went with him a little way, but they soon panicked and warned him that the wolf's bad reputation was certainly justified.

St. Francis told them to stay where they were as he went on to confront the wolf which came snarling toward him in a very threatening manner. He made the sign of the cross and said, "Come here, Brother Wolf. In the name of Christ, I command you to stop hurting people."

Amazing as it may seem, the wolf stopped its charge, closed its mouth, lowered its head, and lay down at Francis' feet as gentle as a lamb.

The saint spoke to it again as it lay there before him. "Brother Wolf, you have frightened these people. You have destroyed God's creatures mercilessly. You deserve to be executed as a murderer. Is it any wonder that this whole town has become your enemy? Brother Wolf, I want to help you to be at peace with them."

The wolf demonstrated that it understood by the manner in which it held its body and tail.

"Brother Wolf, because you are cooperative, I assure you that the people of Gubbio will feed you daily. I know you were hungry and that is why you did those things. In return, you must promise that you will never hurt another living creature. Do you promise that to me?"

The wolf displayed every sign of sorrow such an animal can make, and St. Francis took its paw in his hand. It then followed him meekly back to the town where everyone turned out to meet them. St. Francis preached to the townspeople, telling them that a wolf could only destroy the body and that they had better cause to fear their sins. He concluded his sermon by saying, "Brother Wolf, here before you, has agreed that he will never be a problem for you again. I have promised him that you will give him some food every day so that he will not be required to hunt and kill. I take upon myself the responsibility for the keeping of this agreement."

The wolf lived another two years, going from door to door for a handout of food. It became the town's mascot. Astonishingly, none of the dogs ever so much as barked at it. The people of Gubbio were very sorry when it died, because it was a reminder of the holiness of St. Francis.

BROTHER JUNIPER AND THE PIG'S FOOT

Brother Juniper was one of St. Francis' first companions. He was a very even-tempered and humble man who was never seen to be upset. He achieved such a perfection in self-denial that some people who did not know him well thought he was a little stupid.

Once, when Brother Juniper was visiting a sick friar, he was moved with compassion and offered to do anything he could to help. The sick friar admitted that he would dearly love to eat a pig's foot.

Responding immediately, Brother Juniper said he would get one. Grabbing a kitchen knife, he ran into the fields and caught a pig. He cut off one of its feet and rushed back to clean and cook it. He then served it with much kindness to the sick friar who ate it ravenously.

Unfortunately, the farmer who owned the pig was outraged when he was told what Brother Juniper had done. He stormed in upon the friars, calling them hypocrites, thieves and criminals. He created such a disturbance that St. Francis came forward and apologized, explaining that he was unaware of what had happened. He promised to give him another pig.

But the farmer would not be appeased. In a rage of anger he threatened and cursed the friars, and went away in a huff.

St. Francis then asked Brother Juniper if the charges the farmer had made were true. With innocence of spirit, Brother Juniper told the entire story. The saint was saddened. He said, "Brother Juniper, we are disgraced. The farmer has every right to be angry with us. He will tell everyone in town about what has happened and our reputation will be ruined. Run after him, fall on the ground, and tell him you are responsible. Assure him that you will replace the pig. You have made a serious mistake!"

Brother Juniper was surprised that an act of love could turn out so wrong, but he did not question the assessment or the order. He caught up with the farmer and confessed his guilt, explaining the circumstances. The farmer was still burning with rage and shouted insults at him, calling him a fool, a lunatic, and a criminal.

Since that was not what he expected, Brother Juniper assumed that the man had not understood his explanation. Therefore, he repeated his story and threw his arms around the farmer, explaining that he had done it for love. He was certain the man would agree that he had done the right thing and even suggested that the rest of the pig could be given to the same sick friar.

At that, the farmer was deeply touched by Brother Juniper's simplicity and humility. He knelt down and tearfully expressed his regrets at having been so angry. He confessed that he had not been grateful enough to God for all of his blessings. He then caught the maimed pig, killed, dressed, and cooked it. With much devotion, he brought it to the friars in compensation for the wrong he had done in cursing them.

St. Francis, when he observed the simplicity and humility of Brother Juniper, remarked, "My Brothers, I would like to have a forest of such junipers!"

FRANCIS OF ASSISI: *WRITINGS*
ADMONITIONS

Think of how grand a thing the Lord has done for you! He has created you in the image of his beloved Son, physically, and in his own image, spiritually. And yet all the other creatures under the heaven serve and know and obey their Creator better than you.

If you were smart enough to know all sciences, if you could understand every language, and if you were able to see the stars and planets at close range, you still could take no pride in it. If you were better looking and richer than everyone else, and even if you could work miracles and exorcise demons, none of that would do you any good and neither could it be said to be yours. There is no glory for you in such things. The only thing you can glory in is your infirmities, and in daily carrying of the cross.

Consider the Good Shepherd who suffered crucifixion to save his sheep. And now his sheep must follow him in tribulation and persecution and shame, in hunger and thirst, in temptation and many other ways. In return, the Lord will give them everlasting life.

Often those who sin or experience grief blame their enemy or their neighbor. But this is wrong. You have control over your enemy because your enemy is your body which commits the sins. Blessed is that servant who makes a captive of his enemy and guards himself from it.

No one will ever know the full depth of his capacity for patience and humility as long as nothing bothers him. It is only when times are troubled and difficult that he can see how much of either is in him.

"Blessed are the peacemakers: for they shall be called the children of God." (Matt. 5:9) The genuine peacemakers are those who remain at peace in their souls and bodies when they suffer in this world for the love of our Lord Jesus Christ.

"Blessed are the pure in heart: for they shall see God." (Matt. 5:8) The pure of heart are those who care nothing for earthly things and always look for heavenly things. They never stop adoring and contemplating the living God with a pure heart and mind.

Happy is the person who bears with neighbors, understanding their frail natures, as much as he would want to be borne with by them.

Happy is that devout person who experiences no pleasure or joy except in holy conversation and the works of the Lord, and who uses these means to lead others to the love of God.

Happy is the servant who never speaks because he wants a reward, who always carefully considers what he will say. Unhappy is the religious person who, instead of keeping the good things that the Lord has spoken to him in his heart and demonstrating them by the quality of his life, tries to make it known by talking about it. He may receive nothing more than an earthly reward and his hearers will take away little fruit.

Happy is that brother who loves his brother as much when he is sick and not able to help him as he loves him when he is well and able to carry part of the burden. Happy is the brother who loves his brother as much when he is far away from him as he does when he is close by, and refrains from saying anything about him behind his back that he would not say in his presence.

Where there is love and wisdom, there is neither fear nor ignorance.

Where there is patience and humility, there is neither anxiety nor anger.

Where there is poverty and joy, there is neither greed nor covetousness.

Where there is quiet and meditation, there is neither care nor waste.

Where the fear of the Lord guards the door, the enemy cannot enter.

Where there is compassion and discretion, there is neither excess nor indifference.

RULE OF 1221

[This first set of regulations for the conduct of the Friars Minor presents a simple, but harshly demanding way of life. The three basic requirements are obedience, chastity, and poverty. After giving the details of life together and in relationship with the world, Francis of Assisi then closes with the following exhortation.]

"Love your enemies, bless them that curse you, do good to them that hate you, and pray for them which despitefully use you, and persecute you." (Matt. 5:44) We must follow in the footsteps of our Lord Jesus Christ, who called Judas, his betrayer, a friend and freely laid down his life. Our friends are those who bring suffering, shame, even death to us without provocation. We must love them. We must love them passionately because they are helping us to receive eternal life.

Our base nature, so prone to sin and vice, must be hated. As our Lord says in the Gospel, "For from within, out of the heart of men, proceed evil thoughts, adulteries, fornications, murders, thefts, covetousness, wickedness, deceit, lasciviousness, an evil eye, blasphemy, pride, foolishness: All these evil things come from within, and defile the man." (Mark 7:21–23)

We have turned away from the world and must be careful to obey God's will. We should "let the dead bury their dead" (Matt. 8:22) the way our Lord instructs. We must keep our guard up. Satan will try to turn our minds and hearts away from God by making us think we can have or do something more valuable.

With God's love I urge all my friars to get rid of all attachments and concerns for this world. Serve, love, honor and adore our Lord and God without any idea of looking out for your own interests. Let us make room for God within ourselves that he may come and live with us.

Stick to the words, the life, the teaching, and the Holy Gospel of our Lord Jesus Christ. He has prayed to his Father for us and revealed his name to us, as he said, "Father, I have made you known to those you gave me out of the world. They belonged to you, and you gave them. They have obeyed your word, and now they know that everything you gave me comes from you. I gave them the message that you gave me, and they received it; they know that it is true that I came from you, and they believe that you sent me.

"I pray for them: I pray not for the world, but for them which thou has given me; for they are thine. And all mine are thine, and thine are mine; and I am glorified in them. And now I am no more in the world, but these are in the world, and I come to thee. Holy Father, keep through thine own name those whom thou hast given me, that they may be one, as we are.'' (John 17:9ff)

THE CANTICLE OF THE SUN

[Because of the great beauty of this song in its original Italian, it is presented here with an interlinear free rendering in English.]

Altissimo, onnipotente bon signore,
   Highest One, Almighty good Lord,
Tue so le laude, la gloria, el honore et onne benedictione.
   Yours are the praises, the glory, the honor, and all blessing.
Ad te solo, Altissimo, se konfano,
   To you only, Highest One, do they belong,
et nullu homo ene dignu te mentouare.
   and no man is worthy to mention you.
Laudato sie, Misignore, cum tucte le tue creature,
   I praise you, my Lord, with all your creatures,
spetialmente messor lo frate sole,
   especially mister Brother Sun,
lo quale iorno et allumini noi per loi.
   who brings us the day and illumines us through you
Et ellu e bellu e radiante cum grande splendore
   And he is beautiful and shines with great splendor
de te, Altissimo, porta significatione.
   of you, Highest One, symbolically.
Laudato si, Misignore, per sora luna e le stelle
   Be praised, my Lord, for Sister Moon and the stars
in celu lai formate clarite et pretiose et belle.
   which you formed in heaven, clear and precious and beautiful.
Laudato si, Misignore, per frate vento
   Be praised, my Lord, for Brother Wind
et per aere et nubilo et sereno et onne tempo,
   and for air and storms and calm and all weather,
per lo quale a le tue creature dai sustentamento.
   by which you sustain your creatures.

Laudato si, Misignore, per sor aqua,
>Be praised, my Lord, for Sister Water,

la quale e molto utile et humile et pretiosa et casta.
>who is very useful and humble and precious and pure.

Laudato si, Misignore, per frate focu,
>Be praised, my Lord, for Brother Fire,

per loquale enallumini la nocte,
>through whom you light the night,

ed ello e bello et iocundo et robustoso et forte.
>and he is beautiful and cheerful and robust and strong.

Laudato si, Misignore, per sora nostra matre terra,
>Be praised, my Lord, for sister Mother Earth,

la quale ne sustenta et governa
>who sustains and governs us

et produce diversi fructi con coloriti flori et herba.
>and produces a variety of fruit with colorful flowers and leaves.

Laudato si, Misignore, per quelli ke perdonano per lo tuo amore
>Be praised, my Lord, for those who forgive by your love

et sostengo infirmitate et tribulantione,
>and endure sickness and tribulation,

beati quelli kel sosterrano in pace,
>blessed are they who endure peacefully,

ka da te, Altissimo, sirano incoronati.
>who will be, Highest One, crowned by you.

Laudato si, Misignore, per sora nostra morte corporale,
>Be praised, my Lord, for our Sister Bodily Death,

da la quale nullu homo vivente po skappare.
>from whom no living man can escape.

Guai acquelli ke morrano ne le peccata mortali.
>Woe to those who die in mortal sin.

Beati quelli ke trovarane le tue sanctissime voluntati,
>Blessed are those who are found in your holy will,

Ka la morte secunda nol farra male.
>for the second death cannot harm them.

Laudate et benedicete Misignore et rengratiate
>Praise and bless my Lord and thank him

et serviateli cum grande humilitate.
>and serve him with great humility.

LAWRENCE:
THE PRACTICE OF THE PRESENCE OF GOD

His parents were French peasants, and they named him Nicholas Herman. All the world knows the child born in Lorraine the same year the King James Bible was published (1611) as "Brother Lawrence." From the moment of his profound religious awakening at the age of eighteen until his death at eighty, Brother Lawrence experienced what the Christian hymn begs for—"a closer walk with God."

He was a diamond in the rough—an unordained, poorly educated rustic who was described by his contemporaries as "a great awkward fellow, who broke everything." But it was to this man that droves of other Christians came in search of an authentic devotional experience. Transcriptions of his intimate conversations and sixteen of his letters were gathered into the little collection that bears the title: *The Practice of the Presence of God.* To read the book is to eavesdrop at the curtain that separates the reverent and the profane, the devout and the sanctimonious, the humble and the pharisaical, the pious and the unctuous. Those who came to this barefoot kitchen helper in the Carmelite community at Paris were honestly seeking something they respected. And no doubt many were helped, though some must have sighed, "It is too high. I cannot attain it."

He had his detractors, but so did Jesus Christ. There were those who were put off by his intimacy with God, saying that there must be something wrong with him because ordinary people don't have that kind of experience. Brother Lawrence replied that it was the most natural thing in the world, that he had not performed any magic tricks to discover it, and that anyone who properly ordered his life and mind could share something similar.

There can be no doubt that those who knew him never questioned the authenticity of his spirituality. The man had a warm, close, uplifting, healthy relationship with the Almighty. To spend an hour with Brother Lawrence was a devotional experience.

He had learned the tough lessons of life as a soldier in the Thirty Years War. The brutality that decimated the population of Germany gave him a personal experience of living at its worst. He received a leg wound which left him with a permanent limp and barely escaped being executed as a spy. He emerged from this hellish existence with a deep spiritual longing that led to the awakening he will describe in the pages that follow.

CONVERSATIONS
I.

The first time I saw Brother Lawrence was August 3, 1666. He told me of God's favor when he was converted at the age of eighteen.

He said that it had happened in the winter. The trees were bare, but soon spring would come and the buds would open and there would be new leaves, flowers and fruit. Considering this, he was struck with the powerful care of God, and there began to burn within him a love for God so strong that he could not tell whether or not it had increased any in the forty years that he had loved since that moment. It was as though he had been released from the world.

He said that any of us could have a similar sense of God's presence by keeping up a conversation with God, that we ought to surrender completely to him and seek our happiness in fulfilling God's will, whether that be pain or pleasure.

It was no surprise to him that there was a lot of misery and trouble in the world. On the contrary, he was surprised that there was not more because the world is populated by sinners who are capable of deplorable malice.

He told me that if I were really serious about living the way God intended us to live, I could return for more conversation as often as I liked, and that I would always be welcomed, but if I were merely coming out of curiosity I should not trouble him again.

II.

In our second conversation, almost two months later (September 28, 1666), Brother Lawrence said that he was controlled by love, that he had discarded selfishness, and was determined to make the love of God the purpose of everything he did. It pleased him to pick up a straw from the ground for the love of God.

He said, "The only motive behind my religious life is the love of God. I have tried to do everything for him. Whatever happens to me, whether I am lost or saved, I will continue to act purely for the love of God. This one good thing I will be able to say: Until I die, I shall have done everything I could to love him."

It would not surprise him, since God had already given him such a happy life, that the time would come when he would have to take his turn at suffering. But he assured me that didn't frighten him because he was sure that since he couldn't do it by himself, God would certainly give him the strength to bear it.

He said that whenever he faced any challenge he prayed, "Lord, I can't do this unless you help me." And when he failed, he simply admitted it to God, saying, "I shall never do any better if you leave me to myself. It is you, O Lord, who must prevent my falling." And then he forgot about it.

His life had become simplified since he knew it was his obligation to love God in all things. Since this is what he was trying to do he no longer needed anyone to direct or advise him; what he needed was someone to hear his confessions. He was very aware of his faults, but he was not discouraged by them. He told it all to God and then peaceably returned to his customary practice of love and adoration.

He said that he could never regulate his devotion by the techniques others use. All of the popular mortifications of the flesh and other religious exercises were useless for him. He found it best to go straight to God by a continual practice of love and by doing everything for God's sake.

He also noted that God seemed to have granted the greatest favors to the greatest sinners, and said that the greatest pains or pleasures of this world were in no way comparable with what he had experienced spiritually.

III.

(November 22, 1666) He told me that the basis of his spiritual life was a high regard for God that distracted his attention. He could not recall what he had just finished doing, and hardly noticed his actions when he was doing it. When he left the table, he didn't know what he had been eating. Only one thing was on his mind: the love of God. It was all very simple. He was constantly aware of the loving presence of God.

IV.

He talked with me (November 25, 1666) very fervently and candidly about how he went to God. It all amounts to one big renunciation of everything that does not lead to God, and then becoming accustomed to a continual conversation with him in freedom and simplicity. If we can see that God is intimately present with us, and speak to him every moment, and ask him to tell us what to do when we are not sure, and get busy with it when we plainly see what he requires of us, if we will offer our activity to him even before we do it, and give him thanks when we have done it, we will discover the only secret there is to it.

The depth of our spirituality does not depend upon *changing* the things we do, but in doing for God what we ordinarily do for ourselves.

Our biggest mistake is to think that a time of prayer is different from any other time. It is all one. His view of prayer was nothing other than a sense of the Presence of God. When the appointed times for formal prayer were over, he didn't notice any change. He continued with God, praising and blessing him with all of his energy. The result was that his life was a continual joy, and yet he hoped that God would let him suffer some when he had grown strong enough to bear it.

He said that when we start the spiritual life, we should face squarely who we are. If we did that we would find ourselves contemptible and unworthy of the name "Christian." The truth is that we are bumbling sinners who need to learn a little humility. The greater the perfection a soul aspires after, the more dependent it is upon Divine Grace.

OTHER RECOLLECTIONS OF HIS COMMENTS

He said that when he began his religious life, he spent the hours set aside for private prayer in thinking of God. He wanted to convince his mind and heart of the Divine existence. This meditation took the place of the usual devout sentiments and elaborate ritual. By this short and sure-fire method, he basked in the knowledge and love of God, and resolved to live every moment aware of his presence. He prayed without ceasing.

When he had some job to do he would pray, ''O my God, since you are with me, and I must now obey your command and apply my mind to these outward things, I pray that you will continue to be with me, assist me, receive all my works, and possess all my affections.''

He said, ''We can do *little* things for God. I turn the cake that is frying in the pan for the love of him. And when I have turned it, if there is nothing else to call for my attention I worship God. I have arrived at a state where it is as difficult for me not to think of God as it was at first to get used to it.''

At the end of his recorded conversations, one of his friends wrote: ''As Brother Lawrence had found such comfort and blessing in walking in the Presence of God, it was natural for him to highly recommend it to others. But his example was a stronger inducement than his words. His very appearance was a benediction! Even when he was in the greatest hurry in the kitchen, he still preserved his serenity. He neither rushed nor loafed, but did everything in its turn, with an even composure and tranquility of spirit. 'The time of business,' he said, 'is not different from the time of prayer for me. In the noise and clatter of my kitchen, while several persons are at the same time calling for different things, I possess God in as great tranquility as if I were upon my knees at the Blessed Sacrament.' ''

LETTERS
I. *(Undated)*

My Reverend Mother: Because you want to know how I gained a habitual sense of God's Presence, which our Lord, in his mercy, has seen fit to grant me, I must tell you that I am reluctant to do so. I will agree to it only on the terms that you show my letter to nobody. If I thought that you would let it be seen, I could never write it—as much as I want to help you.

Here is the way it happened: I had read in many books about the various methods of going to God. All of these different ways of practicing the spiritual life confused rather than helped me. What I wanted to know was how to belong entirely to God. I resolved, therefore, to give everything for everything. After having given myself wholly to God, asking him to forgive my sins, I renounced, for the love of him, everything that was not his, and began to live as though God and I were alone in the world. Sometimes I thought of myself before him as a poor criminal at the feet of his judge; at other times I knew him in my heart as my Father, as my God. I worshiped him as frequently as I could, keeping my mind in his holy presence, and calling my attention back to him when it wandered. This wasn't easy. But I kept at it. I made this my business all day long, not just at special prayer times. At all times, every hour, every minute, even in the height of my business, I drove away from my mind everything that was capable of interrupting my thought of God.

While I have not been entirely successful at this, I have still found great advantage in it. When we are faithful to keep ourselves in his Holy Presence, and set him always before us, this not only hinders our wandering, it also gives us a holy freedom. If I may speak like this, let me also say that it gives a familiarity with God. By repeating these acts, they become habitual. The result is that the presence of God is rendered a natural thing.

II.

(June 1, 1682)

You must know that during the forty years and more that I have spent at this, my continual care has been to be always with God, and to do nothing, say nothing, and think nothing which may displease him— and this without any other motive than purely for the love of him.

I am now so accustomed to that Divine Presence that I receive from it continuing nourishment. For more than thirty years my soul has been filled with joys so constant, and sometimes so transcendent, that I am forced to try to moderate them so that they don't show too much on the outside.

If I am sometimes a little too absent from the Divine Presence, as sometimes happens when I am busy, God soon makes himself felt in my soul and calls me back.

God's treasure is like an infinite ocean, and yet a little wave of emotion, passing with the moment, is enough for many. But when God finds a soul filled with a living faith, he pours into it his grace and good favor. They flow into the soul the way a torrent that has been stopped in its course for a while by some debris spreads its pent-up flood.

We often stop this torrent by the little value we give it. Make the most of your opportunity. Redeem the time that is lost. Maybe you don't have much left. Be well prepared for death because you only get one crack at it. Remember, in the spiritual life, not to advance is to go backward.

III. *(1685)*

There is nothing in the world as sweet and delightful as a continual walk with God. Only those who have experienced it can comprehend it. And yet I would not recommend that you seek it because it is so enjoyable. Do it because of love, and because it is what God wants.

If I were a preacher, the one thing I would preach about more than anything else is the practice of the presence of God.

IV.*(November 3, 1685)*

Please get started with this thing. I don't care how old you are. It is better late than never.

I can't imagine how any faithful person can be satisfied without the practice of the presence of God. For my part, I spend as much time as possible alone with him at the very center of my soul, and as long as I am with him I am afraid of nothing, but the least turning away from him is unbearable.

It is necessary to trust God completely. The various forms of devotion, as good as they are, merely help us on our way to God. But when we are already *with God,* they are of little use.

Don't be discouraged if you find this hard to do. When you just try it, you will consider it wasted time. Stick to it! Resolve to persevere in it until the day you die—no matter what!

V. *(Undated)*

I feel sorry for you. It will be advantageous if you can leave your business to others and spend the rest of your life worshiping God. He doesn't lay a great burden on us—

a little thinking of him,

a little adoration,

sometimes to pray for grace,

sometimes to offer him your sorrows,

sometimes to thank him for the good things he does.

Lift up your heart to him even at meals and when you are in company. The least little remembrance will always be acceptable to him. You don't have to be loud. He is nearer to us than you think.

You don't have to be in church all the time in order to be with God. We can make a chapel in our heart where we can withdraw from time to time and converse with him in meekness, humility, and love. Everyone has the capacity for such intimate conversation with God, some more, some less. He knows what we can do. So let's get started. Maybe he is just waiting for one strong resolution on our part. Have courage. We only have a little time to live. You are almost sixty-four and I am nearly eighty. Let's live and die with God.

VI. *(Undated)*

[This letter, addressed to "My Reverend Father," is the longest in the collection. It begins with a summary of the ideas and events already described. Brother Lawrence then goes on to describe "the actual Presence of God—a silent and secret conversation of the soul with God."]

I feel my spirit and all my soul lift itself without any difficulty or effort on my part. It sort of floats in the strength of God. I am sure that some accuse me of inactivity, delusion, and self-love. I admit that it is a *holy inactivity,* and it would be great for self-love if a soul in that state were capable of such. But I can't bear to hear this called delusion, because the soul that enjoys God like this desires nothing but him. If this is my delusion, then God ought to fix it!

VII. *(Undated)*

I don't know what is to become of me. Peace of soul descends on me even in my sleep. I can't imagine what God has in mind for me, or what he keeps me for. I am in such a profound calm that I fear nothing. What can I be afraid of when I am with him? And I try to stay with him, in his presence, as much as possible.

VIII. *(October 12, 1688)*

I admire the strength of our friend. God has given him a good disposition, but he still has a little of the world and a lot of immaturity. I hope his sickness will become God's medicine and make him take stock of himself. It is an opportunity for him to start trusting God.

He should think of God as often as he can, especially when he is in great danger. A little lifting up of the heart will do. A short prayer, one act of inward worship—even while marching into battle—would be entirely pleasing to God. It will also strengthen the soldier's courage.

Tell him to think of God the most he can. Let him get used to this small discipline gradually. No one will notice it, and nothing is easier to do all day long.

IX. *(Undated)*

So you have difficulty with wandering thoughts in prayer! That's nothing new! You have a lot of company.

One way to remedy this is to tell God about it. Don't use a lot of fancy words and make your prayers too long. That in itself will destroy your attention. Pray like a poor, paralytic beggar before a rich man. Make it your *business* to keep your mind in the Presence of the Lord. If you have difficulty with that, don't fret about it. That will only make it worse. Bring your attention back to God in tranquility.

Another way to stay with a prayer is to keep your mind from wandering too far at other times of the day. Keep it strictly in the Presence of God. If you think of him a lot, you will find it easy to keep your mind calm in the time of prayer.

X. *(March 28, 1689)*

Here is my answer to the letter I received from our good Sister. She seems to be sincere, but she is in a bigger hurry than God. Holiness is not achieved all at once.

We can't escape life's dangers without the actual and continual help of God. We need to pray all of the time. And how can we pray to him without being with him? How can we be with him unless we think of him often? And how can we often think of him unless by a holy habit of thought? You tell me I am always saying the same thing. You are right. And I say it because this is the best and easiest method I know, and it is the only one I use. I recommend it to everybody.

We must *know* before we can *love*. In order to *know* God, we must often *think* of him. When we finally love him, we shall automatically think of him all the time, because our heart will be with our treasure.

XI. *(October 29, 1689)*

[This brief letter confesses Brother Lawrence's reluctance to write a man he has been urged to counsel by two women. It closes with a repetition of his constant theme: "Don't forget God. Think of him frequently. Live and die with him."]

XII. *(November 17, 1690)*

I don't pray that you may be delivered from your troubles; rather, I pray that God will give you the strength and patience to bear them. Comfort yourself with him who nails you to the cross. He will let you go when he is ready. Happy are those who suffer with him.

The world doesn't understand this. That's not surprising. They suffer as lovers of the world and not as lovers of Christ. They think that sickness is a pain of nature and find nothing in it but grief and distress. But it can be a consolation to those who understand that God can use illness in mercy.

God is frequently closer to us in sickness than in health. Put all of your trust in him and you will soon be on the road to recovery. Medicine will help you only to the degree God permits. When pains come from God, only he can heal them. Sometimes a disease of the body will cure a sickness in the soul.

Be content with the state in which God places you. I envy you. Pains and sufferings would be a paradise for me if I should suffer with my God, and the greatest pleasures would be hell for me if I could enjoy them without him. It would be the greatest joy of my life to suffer something for his sake.

I must soon go to God. What comforts me now is to see him by faith. And sometimes I see him in such a manner as to make me say, ''I no longer believe, but I *see.*''

XIII. *(November 28, 1690)*

I can't understand how a soul, which is with God and desires only God, can feel pain. Be courageous. Offer your pains to God. Pray for the strength to endure. Above all, develop a habit of conversing often with God. Adore him in your infirmities. At the very height of your suffering, ask him humbly and affectionately—as a child to a good father—to help you to accept his will.

I don't know how God will dispose of me. My happiness grows. The whole world suffers; yet I receive undeserved joy so great I can hardly stand it.

XIV. *(Undated)*

It pains me to see you suffer so long. The only comfort I have is in the knowledge that your grief is a token of God's love for you. Try to see it in this light and you will bear it more easily. I will help you with my prayers, poor as they are.

XV. *(January 22, 1691)*

I thank our Lord for having given you a little relief. I did not pray for any relief, only for strength to suffer with courage, humility, love.

When our minds are filled with God, suffering will become full of sweetness and quiet joy. I know it is difficult to accomplish this. But remember, we can do all things with the grace of God. He never refuses to help those who earnestly ask for it. Knock, keep on knocking, and I promise you that he will open to you in due time and give you what you have wanted for many years. Goodbye. Pray for me as I pray for you. I hope to see him very soon.

XVI. *(February 6, 1691)*

God knows what is best for us, and everything he does is for our good. If we knew how much he loves us, we would accept with indifference the sweet and the bitter.

Let's start being devoted to God in earnest. Let's put everything else out of our hearts. Let's beg this favor of him. If we will do our part, we shall see what changes God can make. I can't thank him enough for the relief he has given you. I hope he will grant me the favor of seeing him within a few days. Let's pray for one another.

[Brother Lawrence became bedridden two days later, and died before a week had passed.]

TERESA OF AVILA:
INTERIOR CASTLE

T eresa of Avila destroys every notion that there are two kinds of religious personalities: active and contemplative. The story of Mary and Martha recorded in Luke 10:38–42, so beloved by every author of spiritual literature, tends to make us think that the two patterns of behavior are clear opposites and mutually exclusive. The Christian is either a Martha, busy with the dishes, or a Mary, sitting at Jesus' feet. Such a simple distinction is simply not true—not even for Mary and Martha all of the time. Most of us combine the characteristics of both, emphasizing one or the other as circumstances dictate or allow. St. Teresa is an outstanding example of a thorough blending of both.

She was born in Avila, Spain in 1515. At the age of twenty-one, Teresa responded to a lifelong urge and became a Carmelite nun in her hometown. As an active Christian, she reformed her Order and founded fourteen monasteries. Her spirit of reform affected the male Carmelites through the cooperation of St. John of the Cross. They used the terms "calced" and "discalced" (with or without shoes) to denote the difference they had brought about. Plagued with very poor health, Teresa somehow managed to attend to a multitude of administrative details. She directed the work of laborers the way a modern contractor hires and oversees employees. She dealt with royalty and "city hall" like a diplomat. She put in an exhausting day that began with worship at five in the morning and often kept her at her desk until well past midnight. A favorite quotation from her autobiography is "Rest? I don't need rest. What I need is crosses!" Another: "I knew I was in for trouble, but now that it was done, I didn't care about that."

It is this same busy, creative, determined administrator who is also one of the greatest contemplative spirits in history. Even while signing contracts or confuting her critics, she was aware that she was living her life in the presence of God. And she would not have us understand that in a figurative sense. She had a personal experience of mystical union with God through a remarkable prayer life that dominated her existence.

All of her writings are worthwhile reading, but it is her *Interior Castle* that may be singled out as her most distinctive creation. In this volume, she ignores the interesting details of her life and work, and concentrates exclusively on her spiritual discoveries. While she is, by nature, a rambling writer who followed her stream of consciousness before the pedagogues knew what one was, *Interior Castle* possesses form and comeliness. Her style remains unsophisticated and direct. To read Teresa is to sit down for a chat with her. She did not read what she had written with a critical eye, scratching out this line and that, amending and shaping, correcting and refining. She simply sat down and wrote what was on her mind, often reminding the reader that she was not very good at it. In fact, she was a wizard at wringing profound meaning from the Spanish language, delicately playing one word against another in puns so subtle that they are often missed by modern translators.

INTERIOR CASTLE
JHS[1]

This is one of the most difficult assignments I have ever been given. I have been ordered to write about prayer. I have little desire to do it. Moreover, for the past three months I have had noises in my head, and I am so dizzy it is difficult to write ordinary business letters. May God, who has helped me with more difficult tasks, help me with this one also.

I begin to write, today, June 2, 1577, at St. Joseph's, a Carmelite monastery in Toledo.

I.

Our soul is like a castle created out of a single diamond or some other similarly clear crystal. There are many rooms in this castle, just as heaven has many mansions.

---

1. Teresa began and ended this work with these letters, the first three in the name, Jesus. It seems appropriate to retain them in this rendering.

How do we enter this beautiful castle? That may seem like a ridic- ulous question. After all, if the castle is our soul, we are already rather intimate with it! But you must try to see that there are many different ways we can exist in this castle. In fact, many remain with the guards in the courtyard outside this castle. They have no desire to enter it and have little concept of what it's like inside.

To the best of my understanding, the doorway into this castle is prayer and meditation. There are those whose prayers are mere mechan- ical repetitions. These poor souls are like the paralytic who waited be- side the pool of Bethesda for thirty years for the Lord himself to come and help him. But there are other souls, busily involved in the affairs of the world, who sometimes, however shallowly, do manage to enter the castle. They come into the reception rooms on the first story. Unfortu- nately, so many reptiles get in through the door with them they are dis- tracted from appreciating what the castle has to offer. But it has been quite an achievement just to get inside.

Before I say anything else, think what a tremendous loss it would be for this splendid castle, this tree of life which is rooted in the Living Waters of God, to fall into mortal sin. That would be the darkest dark- ness of all!

Be patient with me. I don't know what to write. It is not easy to ex- plain things about the interior life. We are told that prayer is valuable and we are urged to pray. There is good advice on how to pray, but very little is said about the supernatural work of the Lord in a soul. It should be helpful, then, for me to describe and explain this heavenly castle in- side us.

I have already mentioned that it has many rooms. Don't think of them as neatly aligned down a hallway. Think of concentric spheres with the palace of the King at the center. Many rooms surround that central core in all directions, layer upon layer. It is impossible to exaggerate the potential of the soul. The Sun at the center illumines all of it. The pray- ing soul must be free to explore this great variety of rooms. It should not hide in a corner. But let it frequently linger in the room of humbling self- knowledge, considering the greatness and majesty of God.

The rooms of this outer level of the Interior Castle are near enough to the surface to still be bothered by the cares of the world. While here, the soul is easily tricked by the Devil. Very little light from the King's palace is perceived this far out. It is difficult for me to explain, but the light is there; it is just hard to see because so many snakes and other wild, poisonous things distract the soul. It's like trying to see the sun with mud in your eyes. To move on to the second level of rooms it will be necessary to get rid of these distractions as much as possible.

II.

The second level is where dwell those who already know how to pray; those who know the dangers of remaining on the first level, but still can't quite free themselves from stepping back into it now and then. They understand that the snakes are bad and try to avoid them. In these second rooms, the Lord's voice can begin to be heard. We remain busy with our jobs and recreation and bargaining, we continue to give in to temptations, but the Lord is able to get through to us. And the attractive things we hear create a tension in us that we would not feel in the first rooms where his voice is drowned out by the noises of the world.

The voice of the Lord is not heard in this second level the way it will be heard when we have penetrated the castle more deeply. Now he speaks to us through other people. Perhaps we hear a sermon or read a book. God has many ways of speaking to us. Perhaps we are sick or in trouble, or pray a brief prayer. His majesty patiently waits for many days, years.

Meanwhile, the devil makes more vicious attacks on the soul in these rooms than in the first ones. Oh my Lord! Your assistance is necessary here. Have mercy and prevent this soul from being led astray right at the beginning! Give it enough light to find its way on into this good castle.

Don't expect anything special, spiritually, at the beginning. Your objective is to lay a foundation. It will rain manna later, when you are in the more interior rooms. Smile with me! We are still beginners, encumbered with thousands of faults and blemishes, our virtues barely able to walk on frail, new legs, and we are looking for favors! His Majesty knows what is best for us. It is not our business to tell him what to give us. The beginner has just one assignment: work hard at making your will conform with God's will. This is important. Don't forget it.

If you stumble, don't give up. God will work something good even out of your fall. The only cure for neglecting to pray is to start praying again.

III.

There is but one thing that can be said to those who, with God's mercy and perseverance, have entered the rooms of the third level: "Blessed is the man that feareth the Lord . . ." (Ps. 112:1) If he doesn't turn back now, he is certainly on the way to salvation.

It is miserable to live under siege, with weapons under the table and beside the bed, always waiting for a surprise attack. It is a blessing to be secure among the blessed.

At this stage there is a strong desire for penance. There is nothing wrong with this, as long as there is no damage done to one's health. But it is not satisfactory to spend too much time here. We have a long way yet to go. The journey requires humility, and a lack of it will detain us in these third rooms for a lifetime. We will be burdened with a load of earthly nature, most of which had been set aside by those who penetrate more deeply into the castle.

It is typical for people who are beginning to order their lives to be easily shocked by others. Perhaps we could learn something from those who shock us. Outward behavior isn't everything. Not everyone will travel the same route. There are many spiritual paths through these rooms. We don't know all of them.

IV.

As I begin to describe the fourth group of rooms, I need to repeat my request to the Holy Spirit that I will be inspired to say something helpful to you. Now I begin to speak of the supernatural.

These beautiful rooms are nearer the King's palace. You may think you will have to be in the other rooms a long time before you can enter here. There is no rigid requirement. The Lord's blessings are his to give when, as, and to whom he will. Since no one has any right to any of them, no one is ever slighted.

It is rare to encounter any poisonous creatures in these rooms. The few that are here are harmless, perhaps even beneficial.

[Teresa's writing in this section becomes exceptionally convoluted as she attempts to express the inexpressible. She knows *what* she wants to say, but she has a difficult time determining *how* to say it. These pages are filled with brief prayers and expressions of exasperation. To be fully appreciated, they must be read in a complete version. The essence of her thought is here imperfectly distilled in words resembling her own.]

Now let me describe the difference between prayerful pleasure and consolations.[2] The one is the result of our meditations and requests made to God; the other begins in God and comes to us. O Jesus, I wish I could explain this! I don't know how to describe the difference I see. There is a verse in the Psalm that ends, ". . . thou shalt enlarge my heart" (Ps. 119:32 KJV). These words will affirm the difference for anyone who has experienced it.

Look at it this way: two ponds of water have quite different sources. One needs elaborate plumbing with canals and pipes. The other is filled with an unseen, continuously flowing spring. The pipes are like our meditations which bring us the water when we have done our work. But the spring is symbolic of the direct gift of God. I can't say where or how it arrives. All I can say is that it begins with God and ends within ourselves, producing a great calm and peace. God enlarges the heart by sending spiritual water from a source deep within us. It is like smelling something cooking on a distant grill. The spiritual joy is not something we can obtain with our own efforts. We can only receive it as a gift. The best way to experience it, then, is not to strive for it. Just love God without any ulterior motives. In humility, recognize that you are not worthy of such an experience. Desire to suffer the way the Lord suffered, instead of seeking spiritual pleasure. We can be saved without these favors. God knows what is best for us. Anyway, how can we make a spring flow water? There is nothing we can do. This experience is given only as God wills and often the recipient is not even thinking about it.

Before I go on, I want to tell you about another kind of prayer which usually precedes this one. It is a supernatural recollection, a di-

---

2. In Spanish, *qustos* and *contentos*.

vine recall. Suppose the residents of this castle have been wandering outside its walls for years. They are not actually traitors; they just are not habitually inside. Now and then they take a few steps toward the door. When the great King sees their good intentions he mercifully wants to call them back in. Like a good shepherd, he makes a call so gentle as to be almost inaudible. But it is enough. They recognize his voice and return. The call of the Shepherd has a powerful effect. They drop those diverting externalities and come back into the castle.

I think that's the best I've ever explained it! I don't know how they hear. It isn't with their ears. But there is a perception of gentle shrinking inside.[3] I have read that it's like a hedgehog or a turtle drawing into itself. The important difference is that it is not done voluntarily, but only when His Majesty grants the favor.

Let me warn you about a danger. Some persons have such weak physical constitutions they are overcome as soon as they feel any interior pleasure. They misinterpret what is happening to them and call the physical experience "spiritual." They figure it must be a rapture. I call it foolishness.[4] It is a waste of time and bad for their health.

When the experiences are given by God there is no withering weakness in the soul, only deep joy at being close to God. It lasts but for a moment of time and there is no external sensation.

I have said more about the rooms in this fourth region because it is fairly common for souls to enter here. The devil can be harmful in this area because the natural and the supernatural are mingled. In the rooms I am yet to tell you about, the Lord doesn't give him much latitude.

V.

How can I ever speak of the treasures and delights that can be discovered in the fifth level of rooms? What can I say? Who can understand? What comparisons are worthy? Enlighten me, my Lord, that I may enlighten your servants.

Most people are able to enter these rooms, but some do so more

---

3. Spanish, *encogimiento*.
4. A typical Teresan pun: *arrobamiento*, rapture; *abobamiento*, foolishness.

consistently than others. "Many are called, but few are chosen." (Matt. 22:14) The experience here is that of an unquestionable union of the soul with God.

Let me illustrate what happens to the soul by comparing it with an example from nature. When spring brings new leaves to mulberry trees, silkworms hatch from tiny eggs. The worms feed on the leaves until they mature. They then spin silk and hide themselves in cocoons. The ugly worm dies and a lovely white moth emerges from the cocoon. This is an astonishing, unbelievable event! If we only heard it repeated as a tale, we would not believe it.

The experiences of the silkworm and the soul are similar. The soul starts to live when warmed by the Holy Spirit and feeds upon the nourishments provided by the Church. When it is mature it spins its silk and begins to build the house in which to die—the house of Christ. I can't quote the verse exactly, but I have heard that our lives are hidden with Christ in God and that real life is Christ.[5]

In the prayer of union, God himself becomes our house. We can weave a little cocoon by eliminating selfishness and any attachment to earthly things, and by practicing the teachings of the Church. Let this silkworm die. Let it die. Dying is what it was born to do. Death fulfills its purpose.

And here is my point: when, in this fifth region of prayer, the silkworm dies to the world, out comes a little white moth. Oh, the greatness of God! Imagine! A soul in this prayer is enclosed in God's greatness for a little while—I think not much more than half an hour—and it is transformed. It no longer recognizes itself. There is now all the difference between an ugly worm and a little white moth. The soul understands it has done nothing to deserve this blessing. All it wants to do now is to praise the Lord. It is willing to die a thousand deaths for him.

Now see the restlessness of this little moth in spite of the fact that it has never been more relaxed in its life. Its problem is that it doesn't know where to land. Every place it sees on earth is unsatisfactory. The food that pleased the worm will not do for the moth. Weaving a cocoon is of no interest when you have wings. Where will it go? It can't return to its beginnings. Though at peace, the soul will feel an inescapable pain

---

5. Cf. Col. 3:3f.

because of this. The only possible solace comes from the realization that God desires it to live in this exile.

As the moth[6] lays new eggs, produces additional silkworms and then dies, so God wants others to benefit from the favors he gives us. It is important, then, to love our neighbors with God's love.

VI.[7]

Now, with the aid of the Holy Spirit, I will tell of the sixth rooms, where the soul wants to be alone with its Spouse. But there will be much conflict before passing on to the seventh mansion.

For instance, there will be a lot of talk. You will be accused of being holier-than-thou, a self-righteous show-off. Friends will desert you. They will say that the devil has led you astray and they will even laugh at you. And if they should praise you, that will be a trial also. Eventually the soul will disregard the praise and find the criticism a joy.

Illness may also become a problem. I know a person[8] who has not been without pain since God granted her this favor forty years ago. There have been other difficulties as well. It seems to me that the Lord allows the devil to try the soul to the point that it thinks God has rejected it.

Suffering like this will enable the soul to enter the seventh rooms. Such hazards only make the moth fly higher.

Consider the ways God awakens the soul. Sometimes, when a person least expects it, His Majesty will awaken it in a flash. Though no sound is heard, the soul is thunderstruck with God's call.

Another way that God can awaken a soul is with an inner voice.[9] They come in great variety. Some seem to come through the ears, others from within the soul. There is danger here. A person under stress may

---

6. Teresa here begins to call the moth a dove. For clarity, the change is not observed in this rendering.

7. In the original, this section of eleven chapters is the longest. The last two sections equal the first five in length.

8. When Teresa uses this phrase, she invariably means herself. It occurs far more frequently in her writings than this rendering would suggest.

9. Locutions.

hallucinate. If melancholy persons report hearing voices, don't upset them by suggesting that they have heard the devil. Play along with them the way you would listen to a sick person. If you try to reason with them there will be no end to the discussion. They will swear that they see and hear things. They are convinced of it.

The inner voice I speak of can come from God, or from the devil, or from one's own imagination. I'll give you some advice. Don't think that you are a better person because you hear this inner voice, even if it is genuinely from God. The only good that results is in how you respond to what you hear. And if what you hear is not in agreement with the Scriptures, pay no attention to it at all.

There are some clues that will help you to determine if God is the source. The first and best indication is in their power and authority. Things are better because it was heard. Some difference is made. For instance, calmness replaces distress. The second sign is a peaceful tranquility in the soul and an eagerness to sing praises to God. The third sign is that the words stick in the memory better than ordinary conversation. There is a strong faith in the truth of what was heard. Even if all the evidence indicates that the soul misunderstood, and much time passes, there is still confidence that God will find his own way to fulfill his promises. Yes, the soul suffers through these delays. There are doubts. One begins to wonder whether these things originated with the devil or the imagination.

The devil will actually prey upon your doubts, fanning the flames. He will especially try to intimidate you if the inner voice spoke of something challenging that will bless others and bring honor to God. It can be very destructive for us to doubt that God can do things that seem beyond our comprehension.

In spite of all these difficulties, there will remain a glowing ember of faith that God will overcome all obstacles and keep his word. Ultimately, the joy of seeing the promise fulfilled will be consoling. With a thousand difficulties overcome, it will see the fulfillment.

Now if the inner voice is only the product of the imagination, none of these signs will be present. There will be no certainty, no peace, no joy. The imagination can take over even when a person is in prayer. A kind of dreaming can occur which has nothing to do with God. Sometimes when we ask the Lord for something, we think we hear what we want to hear. But anyone who has experienced the true speaking of the inner voice will not be deceived. But if the "inner voice" commands an action that will have dire consequences for yourself or for others, don't do anything until you have sought competent counselling.

[The remaining chapters of this section defy a rendering in the present style which can do them justice. They deserve to be read in a complete edition, several of which are listed in the bibliography.]

VII.

You may think that I have said so much about spiritual things that nothing could remain to be said. But just as God is infinite, so are his works. Who will ever tell of all his mercies and wonders? It can't be done! Therefore, everything I have said, and will go on to say, in no way exhausts the possibilities of speaking about God. If it will be of any service to him, may it please His Majesty to guide my pen in order to permit me to communicate something of what God reveals to the souls he brings into this seventh mansion.

O great God! I am reluctant to get into this. Others might think I am speaking from personal experience. I blush with shame. And yet I must not overlook this part. If God is praised and understood a little better, the criticism of the world will not matter. I may even be dead when these words are seen. Blessed be God who lives forever. Amen.

Just as God has a private place in heaven, so does he have a dwelling place in the soul. This seventh room may be considered a second heaven. It is here that a kind of spiritual marriage takes place between God and his spouse, the soul. In this union, God removes the blinding scales from our spiritual eyes and we see the Blessed Trinity with an intellectual vision. The soul sees what we believe by faith.

O God, help me! There is such a difference in hearing and believing these things, and actually being able to perceive and understand the truth of them directly! In the deepest interior place there is first-hand recognition.

You must think that a person who has been permitted entry into this seventh mansion becomes so spiritually absorbed that it is impossible to attend to ordinary responsibilities. On the contrary, there is an intensification of service to God in the world. The person I spoke of found herself greatly improved. Even though she had to deal with many problems and business details, it seemed to her that the essence of her soul remained in that interior room. Part of her soul suffered trials while the other part continued to enjoy peace and quiet with God. It was as though the Martha part complained about the Mary part.

Others may experience this union in another way, but this is how it happened to the person of whom we have been speaking. One day, when she had finished Communion, the resurrected Lord revealed himself in bright splendor, beauty, and majesty. He told her it was time they had a mutual interest in each other's business. He said other things which were understood, but are not to be repeated.

This experience was so different from all the other divine encounters with which she was familiar, it frightened her. It was a powerful, intimate vision. It was a marriage, a union similar to melting two candles together so that they make one flame from one wick. It is like rain mixing with the water of a river—it is all water, inseparable. This must be what Saint Paul means when he says, "He that is joined unto the Lord is one spirit." (1 Cor. 6:17) He also says, "For me to live is Christ, and to die is gain." (Phil 1:21) The soul can repeat these words because this is where the little moth dies joyfully. Christ has become its life.

Now let's see how different this new life is. First of all, there is a total forgetting of self. It is as though the soul no longer has an independent existence. It thinks of nothing for itself and only desires to honor God. Additionally the soul has a new kind of willingness to suffer. Whatever His Majesty orders is acceptable and good. There is no fretting. Persecution brings an inner joy. Hostility toward others is out of the question. One prays for one's enemies.

These effects are not constant in the soul. There is a natural shift within the castle from time to time. Sometimes our Lord leaves us exposed to the venomous snakes in the exterior rooms. The truth of the matter is that those who are nearest Christ are those who have the greatest trials. But if we look at the Crucified One, such difficulties become trifles. We pray, therefore, not for our own pleasure and entertainment, but to find the strength to serve God. Martha and Mary must be joined together.

JHS

I admitted when I began this book that I had little enthusiasm for the task. Now that I have finished it, I confess that I actually enjoyed writing it. I think my readers will enjoy entering this interior castle and roaming through its rooms from time to time.

Yes, there are rooms that are off limits unless the Lord of the Castle invites you in. If you find any doors shut, pass them by. Do not try to force your way in. Aggressiveness angers him; humility pleases him. If you understand that you have no right to enter the third rooms, you will be drawn into the fifth. There you will be able to serve him in such a way that you may eventually be brought to his private dwelling place. Then, when you return, you will find the door always open to you. Learning how to enjoy this castle will allow you to be at peace even when much is demanded of you in the world. You know you can return to a castle that can't be taken away from you.

Remember that although I spoke of seven areas of rooms, there are many others on all sides, above and below. There are lovely gardens and fountains and mazes. You will be moved to praise God for creating such loveliness in his image.

Because I want to be useful in helping you to serve God, I urge you, in my own name, when you read this book, to praise His Majesty and ask him to increase his Church and to enlighten the Lutherans. Pray that he will forgive my sins and release me from Purgatory.

FÉNELON:
MEDITATIONS AND DEVOTIONS

In the days of King Louis XIV, religion became a major preoccupation of the French Court. Men and women of nobility earnestly sought spiritual direction. Some, no doubt, were merely playing at it. Wealthy dilettanti will escape boredom in whatever they can, and even religion can become a chic fad. But many who turned to their priests for personal guidance were honestly seeking a relationship with God that transcended the ordinary. They were willing to devote considerable time and effort to the cultivation of their spiritual life. They were sincerely devout. They were eager to be shown how to improve their living response to God's love.

France produced some outstanding spiritual leaders who satisfied this faithful craving. One of the best was François de Salignac de la Mothe-Fénelon. He was born to an aristocratic family in southwest France in 1651. The sickly child had a weak frame and a brilliant mind. He became familiar with the Greek and Latin classics at an early age and prepared for the priesthood, which he entered at the age of twenty-four.

He wanted to become a missionary to Canada, but frail health made such a strenuous enterprise too risky. He became, instead, a highly respected preacher and spiritual director in his native land and will be remembered as the Archbishop of Cambrai. His acquaintance with Jeanne Marie de la Motte-Guyon, a pious widow who was widely respected for her sometimes over-inflated teachings in Christian mysticism, led to a correspondence that sharpened his own contemplation of the ways of God with the soul.

Fénelon combines human warmth and spirituality with sparkling intelligence and erudition. The things he says feed souls. He touches real life. He possesses a gentle kindness that is like Christ's in its openness and acceptance of human foibles. Long before Jung arrived at his insights into the nature of the human psyche, Fénelon understood that condemnation was oppressive and that the sympathetic understanding of a fellow-sufferer was liberating.

There is no monumental work from his pen that can be singled out for our exclusive attention. To gather the spiritual treasure left to us by this great soul, we must comb through his letters, sermons, and treatises. The sample represented here only hints at the wealth waiting for the reader who will dig deeper.

MEDITATIONS AND DEVOTIONS

Crosses

God is a clever designer of crosses. Some are as heavy as iron or lead. Others are as light as straw. He constructs impressive crosses of gold and jewels. He uses all the things we like best. In spite of their great variety, crosses have two things in common. They are hard to carry and they crucify.

A poor, hungry person bears a leaden cross. But God can bring suffering just as unpleasant to the wealthy. The poor can at least beg for a handout! But the well-to-do have nowhere to turn. And if poor health can be added to the glittering cross the crucifixion is complete. Then we see both our frailty and the worthlessness of our wealth. The things that impress those looking on from the outside are invisible to the ones who possess them. He is being crucified and the world envies his good fortune. Prestige can be more painful than arthritis.

The Use of Crosses

It is hard to believe that a loving God could allow us to suffer. Does it please him? Couldn't he make us good without making us miserable? Certainly he could. God can do anything. Our hearts are in his hands.

But he does not choose to spare us sorrow. In the same way that we are not born instantly mature and have to grow into adulthood, so we must learn to be humble and to trust God. We need our crosses. Suffering can help us loosen some knots that tie us to earth. To resist is merely to delay what God is trying to do for us.

It is not possible for a child to wake from a nap fully grown. God works in the heart the same way he works on the body—slowly, imperceptibly. Physical development is so steady and deliberate we attribute its success to nature and fail to see the hand of God. Similarly, our heavenly Father sends a series of events that wean us from earth by gradual steps. Learning to deny ourselves is a painful process. But the sick soul must take its medicine. Is the surgeon cruel when he makes an incision? No! It is an act of kindness.

The parental heart of God has no desire to hurt us. But he understands that we must get our priorities straight. We cry. We pout. We sigh and groan. We say unkind things about God. He does not intervene. He lets us continue through the process. And we are saved. A little grief has saved us from a much greater sorrow. We can only conclude that God is good, that he is tender and compassionate even when we feel that we have a right to complain that he is unkind.

We suffer. The world ignores us, offends us, is unjust, dangerous and deceitful. But isn't that the same world you are in love with? Your source of sorrow is there!

The Interior Sanctuary

The Scriptures say without hesitation that God's Spirit lives in us, that it gives us life, speaks to us in silence, inspires us, and that it is so much a part of us that we are united with the Lord in Spirit. That is basic Christian teaching. Even those well-educated men who have rejected the notion of an interior life will have to admit it. But they go right on emphasizing the rational. The mind has triumphed over the spirit. They have little use for the Teacher within us.

But the Spirit of God is the soul of our soul! We are blind if we think that we are alone in this interior sanctuary. God is actually more present there than we are. We are constantly inspired, but we suppress this inspiration. God is always speaking to us, but the external noise of the world and the internal churning of our passions confuse us. We can't hear him speaking. Everything around us needs to be silent, and we must be quiet within. We need to focus our entire being to hear this voice. It is a ''soft whisper of a voice'' (1 Kings 19:12), and the only ones who hear it are those who listen to nothing else. It is unfortunate that the soul is so infrequently still. Our selfish desires interfere with the voice within us. We are aware that it is speaking to us. We know that it wants something of us. But we can't understand what it is saying and we are sometimes glad about that.

The inspiration of which I speak is not identical to that of the prophets. They were commanded to speak certain words or to do particular things. On the contrary, this inspiration restricts itself to lessons in obedience, patience, meekness, humility, and the other Christian virtues. It does not tell us to get out there and override the laws of nature or to give divinely authoritative orders to others. It is nothing more than a simple invitation from the depth of our being to be obedient to the will of God. Everything contained in such inspiration is already the accepted doctrine of the Christian Church. Unless your imagination goes to work on it, there will be no addition of temptation or illusion.

Since God is always speaking within us, no one is exempt. He speaks within the most incorrigible sinner. He speaks in the hearts of the scholars who may live clean lives, but who are too full of their own wisdom to listen to God. They depend entirely upon reason. They have a self-inflated notion of their ability. I have often said that any common sinner who is beginning to be converted through honest love of God will understand more about this interior word of the Spirit than those who are set in their own wisdom. God wants to communicate with them, but they are too full of themselves. His presence is with the simple. Who are they? I have not met many. But God knows who they are, and he is pleased to live with them.

Beginners

Those who have lived far from God usually think they are very near him when they finally get started. The peasant thinks he has been to court because he saw the king pass by one day. New Christians give up their worst sins and live a less criminal life. But they are still attached to the world and vainly judge themselves, not by the Gospel, but by their former lives. They compare their today with their yesterday, and they think this is enough to make them saints. They see nothing remaining to be done in order to continue on their path to salvation. Such people have a long way to go. If they had been entrusted with the Gospel in the beginning, it would not be what it is now. It would be much less demanding of us.

*"Pray without ceasing."(*1 Thess. 5:17*)*

What happiness is ours because we can come to our Creator confidently, open our hearts to him, and converse intimately with him through prayer. He wants this. That soul is happy whose prayers are blessed with the presence of God! "Is any among you afflicted? Let him pray." (James 5:13) "Ask, and it shall be given you; seek, and ye shall find; knock, and it shall be opened unto you." (Matt. 7:7) If we had to ask for money in order to get it, how busy we would be in our asking! If by seeking we could find a treasure, we would shovel away a mountain looking for it! If we could get into some high office by knocking at the door, how we would pound away! We will do almost anything for prestige. We will bear any number of crosses to achieve fleeting popularity. We will go out of our way to have some temporary pleasure that leaves nothing to us but remorse.

But we are reluctant to ask for God's favor. And yet, to have it we need only ask for it.

PRAYER

Nothing is more essential for the Christian, or more neglected, than prayer. Most people are not very excited about praying. They find it a tiring ritual which they like to keep as short as possible. Even when one's responsibilities or anxieties lead to prayer, the prayers are often dull and ineffective.

The Christian life is a continual thirsting after God. If you always want to be near God, you will never stop praying.

Many words are unnecessary. To pray is to say, "Thy will be done." (Luke 22:42) To pray is to lift up your heart to God, to be sorry for your weakness, to sigh when you remember your constant stumbling. Prayer of this kind requires no special formula. You don't even have to stop doing whatever it is that is keeping you busy. All that is needed is a movement of the heart toward God and a desire that what you are doing may be done for his glory.

You may complain that you have little interest in prayer, that it bores you, that your mind wanders when you try to pray. If you are not impressed by grand doctrines, or even by the majesty of God who is always near, at least join me in being sorry for your sins.

It may be more difficult for those who are engaged in business to pray and meditate than for those who live in monasteries, but it is also far more necessary. Take some time out for God. Notice how Jesus invited his disciples to a mountain retreat after they had returned from witnessing for him in the cities. If we live and work in a busy place where people talk and behave as though there were no God, it is all the more important that we return to the source of all virtue and restore our faith and love. If he who was without sin prayed without ceasing, how much more should poor sinners like us work at it?

But remember that God listens to what our heart is saying, not our lips. Everything about us must be locked into the prayer. Is there anyone to whom we can speak who should demand more of our attention? Do we think for a minute that he will have any interest in listening to us if we forget what we are talking about when we pray?

Yes, sometimes the most faithful souls will be distracted while praying. They are not always able to manipulate their imagination so that in the silence of their spirits they can enter the presence of God. But spontaneous wanderings of the mind can be overcome. If we make no effort at this we are merely playing at prayer, entertaining ourselves while remaining separated from God.

When you pray, ask for what you will with firm faith. If you are not confident when you pray, little will come of it. God loves the heart that trusts in him. He will never ignore those who place their complete trust in him. St. Cyprian pointed out that when we pray to God, it is God himself who gives us the spirit of our prayer. It is like a Father listening to his child. God dwells deep within us and prompts the prayers.

"Lord, teach us to pray." (Luke 11:1)

Lord, I don't know what to ask of you. You know what I need. You love me better than I love myself. My Father, give your child what he doesn't know how to request. I am afraid to pray either for crosses or for consolations. Here I am before you. My heart is open to you. See what I need. Be merciful to me. Injure me or heal me; cast me down or lift me up. I am fond of your will even when I do not know it. I am silent. I am yours. I yield. All that matters to me is what you want. Teach me to pray. Pray yourself in me.

The Presentation of Christ in the Temple (Luke 2:22–38)

Today Jesus is taken to the temple. The ritual that is given to ordinary children is observed by the Son of God. Divine child, let me join you in your presentation. I want to be carried there in the hands of Mary and Joseph. I want to become a child like you. You made a poor boy's sacrifice—a pair of doves. Immortal King, in time to come you will not have anywhere to lay your head. You enrich the world with your poverty. You appear at the temple as a child of poor people.

Blessed are those who become poor with you. Blessed are those who have and desire nothing. Blessed are those who surrender everything to you at the foot of your cross, who no longer claim their own hearts, who have no desires of their own, who belong to you. This is a luxurious poverty, an emptiness that is more full than the world's greatest vault.

It is hard to understand the truth that we are separated from God until we abandon ourselves and become lost in him.

What will matter when I am no longer of any concern to myself? I will think less about what happens to me and more about God. His will be done. That is sufficient. If enough self-interest remains to complain about it, I have offered an incomplete sacrifice.

It isn't easy. Old ways of thinking and behaving do not vanish at once. Every now and then they spring back to life. I begin to mutter, ''I didn't deserve such treatment! The charges are false and unfair! My friend is letting me down! I have lost everything! No one comforts me! God is punishing me too severely! I expected some help from those good people, but they are ignoring me! God has forsaken me!''

Weak and trembling soul, soul of little faith, do you want something other than what God wills? Do you belong to him or to yourself? Renounce the miserable self in you. Cut every string. Now you are getting down to the business of sacrifice. Anything less is child's play. There is no other way your two doves can be offered to God.

O Jesus, I offer myself with you. Give me the courage I need to completely renounce myself. Your doves did not spare you your cross.

Your presentation in the temple was but the beginning of what ended at Calvary. None of the offerings I can make will ransom me. I must give myself even to the point of dying on a cross. It is nothing to lose luxury, fame, money, life. We must lose ourselves in you.

Whitsunday

Lord, you began to perfect your Apostles by taking away from them the very thing they didn't think they could do without—the actual presence of Jesus. You destroy in order to build. You take away everything in order to restore it many times over. This is the way you work. You do it differently than we would do it.

Once Christ was gone, you sent the Holy Spirit. Sometimes lacking is more powerful than having. Blessed are those who are deprived of everything. Blessed are those from whom Jesus is removed. The Holy Spirit, the Comforter, will come to them. He will comfort their sorrows and wipe away their tears.

But, Lord, why isn't my life filled with this Spirit? It ought to be the soul of my soul, but it isn't. I feel nothing. I see nothing. I am both physically and spiritually lazy. My feeble will is torn between you and a thousand meaningless pleasures. Where is your Spirit? Will it ever arrive and "create in me a clean heart, O God?" (Ps. 51:10) Now I understand! Your Holy Spirit desires to live in an impoverished soul.

Come, Holy Spirit! There is no place emptier than my heart. Come. Bring peace.

The Holy Spirit floods the soul with light, recalling to our memory the things Jesus taught when he was on earth. We find strength and inspiration. We become one with Truth. It is no longer outside of us, but a part of our being.

The Spirit of love teaches without using any words. There is neither sound nor gesture, but all becomes light. There are no demands, but the soul is prepared in silence for every sacrifice. Once we have experienced holy love we are no longer satisfied with any other love. Unspeakable joy becomes ours without any effort on our part! Love is now a fountain that flows through us.

O my Love, my God! Glorify yourself in me. My only joy in life is in you. You are everything to me.

Divine Illumination (From "Proofs of the Existence of God")

There is a spiritual sun that illumines the soul with greater intensity than the physical sun which shines on the body. It casts no shadows and never leaves half of the earth in darkness. It is as bright at night as it is in the day. It exists within us. No one can block any of its light. There is no place we can go to escape it. It never sets. The only clouds that can obscure it are our emotions. It is a glorious day. It shines on a primitive person in a dark cave. Even a blind person walks in its light.

Human theories are plausible in proportion to their agreement with this inner teacher. We listen to all the rational arguments and then we consult this oracle and accept its judgment. I laugh when I am told that a part is equal to the whole. I consult with my inner teacher and remain unconvinced.

This light within us is superior to us. We may deny it and ignore it, but if we pay attention to it there is no way we can contradict it. I appear to have two kinds of reasoning abilities. One is my own; the other is given. My own is flawed, rash, unpredictable, obstinate, ignorant, narrow. The other is perfect, constant, eternal, inexhaustible. How do I put my finger on this reason that is given from without? Where is it? It is so near and yet so far. It is God himself!

Advice to a Seeker

Christian perfection is nothing to dread. There is pleasure in giving ourselves to one we love. There is a contentment which you will never discover by giving in to your passions, but which will certainly be yours if you give yourself up to God. It is not the satisfaction of the world, but it is nonetheless genuine. It is a quiet, calm peace. The world can neither give it nor take it away. If you have any doubt about it, try it yourself. "Oh, taste and see that the Lord is good" (Ps. 34:8 KJV).

Organize your time so that you can find a period every day for reading, meditation and prayer. This will become easy when you truly love him. We never wonder what we will talk about. He is our friend. Our hearts are open to him. We must be completely candid with him, holding nothing back. Even if there is nothing we care to say to him, it is a joy just to be in his presence. Love is a far better sustainer than fear. Fear enslaves, but love persuades. Love takes possession of our souls and we begin to want goodness for itself. God is a kind and faithful friend to those who sincerely become his friend.

Knowing God

It is odd that we do so little for God, and that such little as we do is done so reluctantly. We do not know him. We are willing to deny his existence. If we say we believe in him, we have done little more than bow to common consent. We have no living conviction of God. We admit that he is, but we avoid finding out for ourselves. Our thoughts about God are vague. He is mysterious, unknowable, far away. We conceive of him as a powerful being who demands much of us, who does not want us to have a good time, who threatens us with natural disasters, and who has a very low opinion of our worth. Of a person who thinks like this it can be said that he "fears God." But he only fears him. He does not love him. A student fears the schoolmaster's ruler; a slave dreads the blows of his overlord. But wouldn't you prefer the service of a loving son?

People think as they do because they do not know God. If they knew him they would love him. "He that loveth not, knoweth not God; for God is love." (1 John 4:8) The person who only fears God cannot be said to know him.

O God, if I only think of you as an omnipotent being who created everything and made the laws of the universe, I do not know you. I only know a part of you, and *that* not the best part. There is also about you that which transports and dissolves my soul. When I discover this aspect of your being I can say that I know you are the God of my heart.

You are always with me. When I sin, you hold it before me, making me sorry, inspiring me to do better, and offering me your pardon with outstretched arms. Any good that I do is done by you through me and I lose touch with such good deeds as soon as I take credit for them.

I consider the wonders of nature in order to obtain an image of your glory. I seek evidence of you among your creatures. I forget to look for you in the depths of my own soul. There is no need to go down into the depths of the earth or to travel beyond the seas or to ascend into heaven to find you.[1] You are nearer to us than we are to ourselves.

O God, you are so glorious and still you are intimate, so high and

---

1. An allusion to Ps. 139:8ff.

yet so low, so enormous and yet within me, so awesome and yet worthy of love. Will your children ever cease being so ignorant of you? When we counsel others to look for you in their own hearts they are as mystified as if we had told them to look for you in some unexplored territory in a distant land. For a worldly person there is no place more remote, more unknown, than the depths of his own heart. He does not know what it means to enter into himself. He has never tried it. He can't even imagine that he possesses such an inner sanctuary in the impenetrable regions of his soul where you can be worshiped in spirit and in truth.[2]

My Creator, I can close my eyes and shut out all exterior things which are nothing but pointless irritations to the spirit. Then, in the depths of my heart, I can enjoy an intimacy with you through Jesus, your Son.

O God! We don't know who you are! "The light shineth in darkness" (John 1:5) but we don't see it. Universal light! It is only because of you that we can see anything at all. Sun of the soul! You shine more brightly than the sun in the sky. You rule over everything. All I see is you. Everything else vanishes like a shadow. The person who has never seen you has seen nothing. He lives a make-believe life. He dreams.

But I always find you within me. You work through me in all the good I accomplish. How many times I was unable to check my emotions, resist my habits, subdue my pride, follow my reason, or stick to my plan! Without you I am "a reed shaken in the wind." (Matt. 11:7) You give me courage and everything decent which I experience. You have given me a new heart which wants nothing except what you want. I am in your hands. It is enough for me to do what you want me to do. For this purpose I was created. Command, forbid. What do you want me to do? What do you want me to refrain from doing? Whether I am lifted up or cast down, comforted or suffering, working for you or doing nothing worthwhile, I continue to love you. I yield my will to you. With Mary I say, "Be it done unto me according to thy word." (Luke 1:38)

Before Easter's Dawn

Now I will think about Jesus in that time between his death on the cross and his resurrection. For him, the one will be as real as the other,

---

2. Cf. John 4:23.

a translation from earthly life to eternal life. O my Savior, I love you! I worship you in the tomb. I enter it with you. I have no desire for the world to pay any attention to me. I don't even care to be conscious of myself. I go down into the darkness and the dust. I am not among the living. I am dead. The life which is being prepared in me is now hidden with Christ.

This is a strange moment. Not many would want to join me now. But how is this different from baptism? The Apostle wrote: "Therefore we are buried with him by baptism into death: that as Christ was raised up from the dead by the glory of the Father, even so we also should walk in newness of life." (Rom. 6:4) What is this death which is so necessary to Christian character? Where is this tomb? It is in our hearts.

Sadly, I have always desired to impress others. I want their approval. I need to feel loved. I crave popularity. I attempt to win my neighbor's hearts. It would be better to steal the incense that is glowing on God's altar than to try to capture what belongs only to God.

O God, when will I stop wanting to be loved? When will I cease being so eager for applause? All love and glory belong to you. I am ashamed of my desire for appreciation. Lord, punish my pride. I stand with you against myself. I take the side of your glory as opposed to my vanity.

Selfish man! In love with yourself! How could you be worthy of any tenderness or affection apart from God?

Lord, I no longer need to be loved. The more sensitive I am in demanding the love of others, the less I deserve their love. As for the applause of others, you can give it or take it away as it pleases you. I want to become indifferent to such things. If there is anything in my reputation that will bring you glory, that is all right. But let me care nothing about it. As long as any secret need to be approved and respected remains in me, I am not dead with Christ and will not be able to enter his resurrected life.

The errors of the old man must be buried. Everything must die. Everything must be sacrificed. But it will be returned with interest. When we have lost all that is in us, we shall recover it all in God. Our love will grow until it becomes like the love of God.

Lord Jesus, you died to help me die. Take my life. Don't let me hesitate. I draw no protective line around anything that needs to go.

FRANCIS DE SALES:
INTRODUCTION TO THE DEVOUT LIFE

F rancis de Sales was bishop of Geneva during the lifetime of many first generation Calvinists. His gentle, patient, honest spirituality was a valuable asset to all Christians during those turbulent years. Like Francis of Assisi, he was not the kind of personality that would invite any kind of hostile exchange. His warm humanity radiates from every page of his voluminous writings.

His *Introduction to the Devout Life* began as a series of letters of guidance to Mme. de Charmoisy, wife of the ambassador of the Duke of Savoy. She was so impressed with his instruction that she showed it to the rector of the College of Chambery. He shared her estimate of the value of the material and urged de Sales to have it published. He made a few minor revisions such as addressing the reader as "Philothea" (Lover of God). It was published in 1609 and was immediately recognized as one of the truly great masterpieces of devotional literature.

While the author makes no claim for any originality of thought, he does admit that he has brought everything together in a fresh way. In fact, his careful style and his constant awareness of the limitations of his readers, combined with a unique talent for apt illustration, make this work far and away the best of its kind. Others have said some of the same things, to be sure, but none of them have said them in *this way,* and with such symmetry and naturalness.

In a letter which is now printed under the title *On the Preacher and Preaching,* de Sales commented upon the value of illustration, or "comparisons." He wrote, "They have great power to aid understanding and motivate the will." He applauds Christ's ability to teach great truth with something as simple as seeds. His own references to nature, sometimes more fanciful than factual, make the *Introduction* sparkle with life.

In that same letter he also warns against the use of substandard material. "The preacher must be careful not to tell about false miracles and nonsensical tales which are common enough in popular books. Such things will make us deserve scorn and criticism." Regarding the lives of the saints, he said, "What could be more helpful? What is a life of a saint other than the Gospel being practiced? The written Gospels have the same relationship to saintly lives that notes have to music."

One of the features of the *Introduction* is its insistence upon using the services of a spiritual director. One of his early biographers, Jean Pierre Camus, discussed this topic with him personally, and we are privileged to have de Sales' own amplification of the concept as you will meet it in the pages that follow. Camus wrote, "I once asked Francis who his Spiritual Director was. He pulled *Spiritual Combat* from his pocket, explaining, 'This little book has been the Director of my inner life since I was young.' I reminded him that in his *Introduction* he wrote of having a living Director. 'You are correct,' he said, 'but remember that I also said he would be difficult to find. We can look for guidance among the books of authors who are no longer living. Devotional books are out best Directors. But when we can't understand what we read we should consult with those who are familiar with the language of the mystics. But there is no advantage to always consulting with the same individual. As the Scripture says, "In the multitude of counselors there is safety." (Prov. 11:14)' "

INTRODUCTION TO THE DEVOUT LIFE

Others who have written about devotion directed their thoughts toward those who have withdrawn from ordinary life. It is my intention to teach those who live in ordinary families and communities. Because many such people think it cannot be done, they never attempt living devoutly. No doubt, it *is* difficult, but I want to help anyone who will try it.

I.

As a Christian, Philothea, you will want to live a life of devotion because you know it will please God. True devotion must be sought among many counterfeits. People naturally think their way is best. The person who fasts thinks this makes him very devout, even though he may harbor hatred in his heart. Another is a total abstainer from drink who tricks and cheats his neighbor, drinking, as it were, his neighbor's blood. Another is sure he is devout because he says many prayers, and yet his language is arrogant and abrasive at home and at work. Another gives liberally to the poor, but is unable to forgive his enemies. Another forgives his enemies but doesn't pay his bills. All of these could be thought of as devout, but they are not. They only hint at devotion.

Genuine devotion is simply honest love of God. When this love becomes so much a part of us that we automatically do deliberate good, then it can be labeled "devotion." Ostriches are not flying birds, chickens fly short distances with much effort, but eagles, doves, and swallows fly high and far. Sinners are like the ostrich and are earthbound. Good people who have not quite reached devotion are like the chicken. They fly in God's direction, but inefficiently and awkwardly. The devout soar to God with regularity. Devotion, then, is a natural agility of the spirit.

The Israelites were discouraged from entering the Promised Land by reports of the hazards that waited there for them. They were told that the air was bad and that the natives were monsters. In the same way, dear Philothea, the world makes noises about holy devotion. It says the devout are long-faced and gloomy. It can only see the outward evidence of prayer, fasting, acts of charity, suppressed anger and passions, self-denial and other things which may seem painful, as such. It can never see the warmth of inward devotion that transforms such difficult things into joy, just as the bees turn the bitter nectar of thyme into honey. Devotion is a kind of spiritual sugar that removes bitterness from life's experiences.

As God commanded the various plants to bear distinctive fruits, so does he command Christians to express a devotion that is proper for individual circumstances. Devotion will take different forms among executives and laborers, young girls and widows. Devotional practice must be tailored to the individual.

Aristotle pointed out that the bee does no harm to the flower when it extracts honey. Not only does true devotion bring no harm to your secular occupation, it actually enhances it. Every kind of work becomes more pleasant. It is heresy to think that the devout life cannot be practiced by soldiers, mechanics, politicians, and all kinds of ordinary people. Wherever we are, whatever we do for a living, we can and should desire to live a devout life.

If you are serious about this, it is very important for you to find a good spiritual director, a faithful friend who can answer your questions and guide you along the proper path. Make your choice carefully. Not one in ten thousand is worthy. Ask God to lead you to such a person, and when you find your own, thank God and be on your way together.

The first step toward the devout life is the cleansing of your soul. "Then be done with your old self . . . become someone new . . ."* (Eph. 4:22–24) Remove anything that stands in the way of your union with God. This will be a gradual process. It has been compared with sunrise which brings light in imperceptible steps. A slow cure is best. Have courage and patience, Philothea. It would be a pity to become discouraged and give up because you see so many imperfections in yourself. However, the opposite, thinking that you are already perfect after the first day of throwing away things from your old life, is worse. It's like trying to fly without wings. Actually, the work of cleansing your soul will go on for a lifetime. Our perfection consists of struggling against our imperfection.

The First Cleansing

The first cleansing must be a confession of sin. Be honest and recall in detail every sin of your life. Write them down if you want. And then with great sorrow admit that you have fallen from grace, given up heaven, chosen hell, and rejected God's love. What I am asking for, Philothea, is a general confession of a lifetime of sin. This is the way to see who you are. It will bring healthy regret for past errors, and fill us with gratitude for God's mercy. We will see how patiently he has been waiting for us, and that will calm us and make us want to do better.

The Second Cleansing

All of the Israelites left Egypt, but in the desert many of them had second thoughts and wanted to return. In the same way, some resolve to avoid sin, but they look back at Sodom even while fleeing it. Like a sick man who has been told by his doctor to eliminate melons from his diet, they give up their sins, but go right on talking about them, desiring them, and envying those whose diets are not restricted. Philothea, if you want to live a devout life you are required both to stop sinning and to lose your appetite for it.

To arrive at this, meditate in the manner outlined below. With God's help, these steps will pluck both the sin and the desire for it out of your heart. Follow the order I have given them, one a day. It is best to do this in the morning, and then reflect upon them during the remainder of the day. If you are not familiar with meditating there is some help for you in the second part.

1. Meditation on Our Creation

PREPARATION:

Place yourself in God's presence.

Ask him to inspire you.

THOUGHTS:

Think of the time before you were born. Where was your soul then? The world existed, but it saw nothing of you.

God pulled you out of that void and made you who you are out of his own goodness.

Think of the possibilities God has placed in you.

RESPONSES AND RESOLUTIONS:

Be humble before God. "Oh my soul, you would still be a part of that nothingness if God had not pulled you out of it. You would have neither consciousness nor activity."

Thank God. "My good Creator, I owe you a tremendous debt. You made me what I am. How can I ever express my thanks?"

Reprimand yourself. "I have run far away from my Creator and sinned. I have not respected his goodness. Beginning now, I will admit that I am nothing. How can dust and ashes take pride in itself? I want to change my life. I will follow my Creator."

CONCLUSION:

Thank God. Offer yourself to him. Ask him to help you keep your resolutions.

When you have finished your prayer, go back through it and pick a few flowers. Make a devotional nosegay, a spiritual bouquet to enjoy all day long.

2. Meditation on the Purpose of Life

PREPARATION:
>Place yourself in God's presence.
>Ask him to inspire you.

THOUGHTS:
>God did not put you in the world because he needed you. He made you for the purpose of working his goodness in you by giving you his grace. He has given you a mind to know him, a memory to recall his favors, a will to love him, eyes to see what he does, a tongue to sing his praise, etc.
>
>This is the reason you are here. Anything that hinders it must be avoided.
>
>Think of the unhappy people who miss this point and live as though they were here only to construct houses, plant trees, accumulate money, and waste themselves on the trifling.

RESPONSES AND RESOLUTIONS:
>Scold your soul with humility. Remind it that until now it has been so miserable that it hasn't thought much about these things. Ask yourself, "What did I think about when I did not think about God? What did I remember when I forgot God? What did I love when I did not love God?"
>
>Hate your previous behavior. "I am through thinking shallow thoughts and making futile plans. I renounce bad friendships, ugly deeds, and self-indulgence."
>
>Turn to God. "My Savior, from now on you will be the only thing I think about. I will stop thinking about evil things. I will remember your mercy toward me every day. The vanities I used to chase after now disgust me."

CONCLUSION:

Thank God for your purpose in life. Ask him to help you to measure up to it.

Pick some spiritual flowers.

3. Meditation on God's Blessings

PREPARATION:

Place yourself in God's presence.

Ask him to inspire you.

THOUGHTS:

God has blessed you with a body and everything necessary to sustain life. Think of those less fortunate than yourself.

Think about the clarity and capacity of your mind. God has blessed you. Remember that some are not so fortunate.

Think about your spiritual blessings. Philothea, you grew up in the Church. You have heard about God from childhood. Notice the small things and see how gentle and kind God has been in your life.

RESPONSES AND RESOLUTIONS:

Let God's goodness astonish you. "How good God has been to me! How merciful! How generous!"

Let your gratefulness astonish you. "Why did you care about me, Lord? I am not worthy. I have thrown your blessings away like so much trash. I have not been thankful for it all."

Declare a resolution. "I resolve to stop being unfaithful, ungrateful and disloyal to God."

Go to church. "I will pray and observe the sacraments. I will hear your holy word and make it a part of my life."

CONCLUSION:

Thank God for what you see now. Offer your heart to him. Ask him to help you keep your promises.

Pick a little spiritual bouquet.

4. Meditation on Sin

PREPARATION:
>Place yourself in God's presence.
>Ask him to inspire you.

THOUGHTS:
>Remember when you first began to sin and how your sins increased over the years. Think about your sins toward God, yourself, your neighbors. Think about the things you have done, spoken, desired, fantasized.
>Think about how lightly you have handled holy things, and how you have run to escape God even as he was looking for you.

RESPONSES AND RESOLUTIONS:
>Let this trouble you. "Dear God, how can I let you see me? Not one day of my life is spotless! Is this how I pay you back?"
>Ask God to forgive you. "Like the prodigal son, like Mary Magdalene, I throw myself down before you and ask for mercy on a sinner, my Lord."
>Promise to live a better life. "With your help, Lord, I will not sin again. I hate my sin. I will admit each sin and drive it out of my life. I will start by weeding out the most troublesome. I will make amends where I can."

CONCLUSION:
>Thank God for patiently waiting for this moment. Offer your heart to him. Ask him to let it be as you have promised. Seek his strength.[1]

5. Meditation on Death

PREPARATION:
>Place yourself in God's presence.
>Beg for his grace.
>Imagine yourself bedridden with a terminal illness.

---

1. Note that no reference is made to a spiritual nosegay, and notice also the bouquet at the conclusion of the next meditation.

THOUGHTS:

Think of the unpredictability of the time of your death. You don't know whether it will be summer or winter, day or night. Will it come suddenly or with time to prepare? Will it result from sickness or accident? You know nothing about what will kill you or when it will happen. All you know is that you *will* die.

Think how that will remove you from the world. All the little recreations of life will evaporate. Only God will be important. Small sins will loom like mountains, and your devotion will seem very small.

Think about your soul saying goodbye to your money, your clubs, your games, your friends, parents, children, husband, wife, everyone. See it say goodbye to your body lying there ugly with the pallor of death upon it.

Think of the speed with which others will take that lifeless body out to be buried. And when that job is done, consider how little the world will ever think of you again. It will remember you no more than you have thought of others who have died.

Think about where your soul will go after leaving your body. Which path will it take? It will travel the same road it started to travel in this world.

RESPONSES AND RESOLUTIONS:

Run to God and let him hug you. "Lord, look out for me when I die. Make it a good experience."

Have no attachment to this world. "World, you are nothing ultimate for me. I have no permanent relationship with you."

CONCLUSION:

Thank God. Offer your desires to him. Ask him to make your death happy in Christ.

Gather a bouquet of myrrh.

6. Meditation on Judgment

PREPARATION:

Place yourself in God's presence.
Ask him to inspire you.

THOUGHTS:

When earthly time has run out, this planet will be reduced to ashes by a raging fire. Nothing will escape.

Think about the frightening words Scripture speaks to the evil, "Depart from me, ye cursed, into everlasting fire, prepared for the devil and his angels!" (Matt. 25:41)

Think about the opposite command that is spoken to the good, "Come, ye blessed of my Father, inherit the kingdom prepared for you from the foundation of the world!" (Matt. 25:34)

RESPONSES AND RESOLUTIONS:

Let these thoughts trouble you deeply. "O God, who will make me secure on the day of judgment?"

Judge yourself—now. "I will look for those things that stain my conscience and condemn them for you in advance, O Lord. I will confess my sins."

CONCLUSION:

Thank God. Offer him a penitent heart.

Gather a bouquet.

[The remaining four meditations on Hell, Paradise, Choosing Heaven, and The Deliberate Decision To Live a Devout Life continue the pattern already established. They are no less important than the first six, and are vital parts of a spiritual process. Again, it is hoped that this condensation will prompt you to seek a complete version of this magnificent work. The meditations end with what can be termed the "theme song" of the book: "With this blessed chorus I continually proclaim my decision—Live, Jesus! Live, Jesus!"[2]]

How To Confess Everything

The poison of a scorpion can be turned into its own antidote. Sin is bad, but it can become better when distilled by confession and repentance. Simon called Mary Magdalene a sinner, but our Lord disagreed. He was pleased with her humble act of anointing him with expensive

---

2. *"Vive, Jésus! Vive, Jésus!"*

perfume. When we are sorry for our sin, we honor God and such sins become sweet and pleasant.

It is important to tell the doctor exactly what are our symptoms. In confessing sin, be certain to tell it all, candidly and sincerely. This will greatly relieve your conscience. Then listen obediently for any guidance. After your general confession, make the following contract with God. Spend some time meditating upon it before you sign it.

A Contract Between My Soul and God

In God's presence, aware of his mercy to me, acknowledging my unworthiness and my indebtedness, I confess the sin I abhor and humbly ask for grace and pardon. This is the only hope I have. I renew my vow of faith and renounce all evil. I resolve to serve and love God forever. To him I dedicate my mind, my heart, my body. If I should succumb to temptation and fail to keep this contract, I will, with the help of the Holy Spirit, stop as soon as I see what is happening and return to God's mercy without delay.

This is my desire and my resolution. I sign it now without reservation or exception.

_____

(signed)

Almighty God, help me to keep this sacrifice of my heart. As you have inspired me to do this, give me the strength to keep it. Live, Jesus!

Finishing the First Cleansing

After you have done the above, listen inwardly for the Savior's assurance of pardon as you are absolved. Experience the joyous celebration of the angels in heaven.

In a moment I will give you some instructions which will help keep you from future sin, but first let me describe the total cleanliness we desire.

The low angle of the sun early in the morning reveals the wrinkles of our faces. In a similar manner the Holy Spirit lights our consciences and we see our sins more distinctly. No doubt you can see that you still have some proclivity to sin. We are never entirely free from these tendencies, but we can stop having affection for them. It is not the same to lie occasionally in some unimportant banter as it is to enjoy lying habitually about serious matters.

Spiders are not deadly to bees, but they entangle their honeycombs with webs and make their work difficult. Excusable sins will not kill your soul, but if they wrap a tangle of bad habits around you, devotion will suffer. Philothea, it is not earthshaking to tell a small lie, or to say or do something slightly risqué, or to dress, joke, play, or dance with a little freedom—as long as you don't allow these spiritual spiders to spin their webs and ruin the hive of your conscience. While it is not illegal to have a little harmless fun, it can become dangerous. The evil is not in the pastimes; it is in our affection for them. Don't sow weeds in the soil of your heart. Your garden space is limited.

Evil habits can corrupt the best person, but God's grace (if we cooperate) can improve the worst. Here, then, are the instructions that will show you how to get rid of your desire for them.

II.

Prayer Is Necessary

Prayer is the most effective means at our disposal for the cleansing of our mind and emotions. This is because it places the first in God's bright light, and the other in his warm love. Prayer is like water that makes plants grow and extinguishes fires.

Best of all is silent, inward prayer, especially if it reflects upon our Lord's loving sacrifice. If you think of him frequently, he will occupy your soul. You will catch on to his manner of living and thinking and will begin to live and think like him. It is exactly like the way children learn to talk by listening to their mothers and then make sounds with their own voices.

Philothea, there is no other way in. Prayer is essential. Find an hour each day, in the morning if possible, and pray. Try to do this in the sanctuary of a church if you can. This will prevent interruptions.

Start every prayer in the presence of God. Be strict about this and you will soon see its value. Don't rush through your prayers. The Lord's Prayer said once with comprehension is better than many prayers said in haste.

There are other aids to prayer (such as the rosary) that can be helpful if you know how to use them correctly. But if you can do it, inward, silent prayer is best. If you are reciting a standard prayer and find your heart being drawn deeper, by all means leave the one and go after the other. Don't worry about leaving your spoken prayer unfinished. Your silent prayer pleases God the most, and it will be better for your soul.

Be diligent about this. Don't let a morning pass without some time in silent prayer. But if the demands of business or some other responsibility prevents it, then be sure to repair the damage that evening. And make a vow to start your regular practice of morning prayer again tomorrow.

A Simple Way To Meditate

Perhaps you are not able to pray silently. Many people today are poor at this. Here is an easy way to get started.

Let me explain the part I have called "preparation," in which I instruct you to place yourself in God's presence and ask him to inspire you. There are several ways you can place yourself in God's presence.

1. Consider how God is present in all things and in all places. Wherever the birds fly, they are constantly in the air, wherever we go God is always there. Instead of merely assenting to this, it is necessary to make the realization of its truth live for us. Since we can't see God physically present, we need to activate our consciousness. Before praying it is necessary to remind ourselves of God's actual presence. A good way to do this is with Bible verses. "If I ascend up into heaven, thou art there. If I make my bed in hell, behold thou art there." (Ps. 139:8) "Surely the Lord is in this place; and I knew it not . . . How dreadful is this place! This is none other but the house of God, and this is the gate of heaven." (Gen. 28:16–17)

2. Remember also that God is not only where you are, he is also actually in your heart, in the core of your spirit. "For in him we live, and move, and have our being . . ." (Acts 17:28)

3. Think about our Savior watching his children at prayer. "Look! He is standing there by the wall. He is looking in the windows and gazing through the lattice."* (Song 2:9)

Asking God to inspire you is a prayer of invocation. You already know God is present. Now your soul bows before his majesty and asks for help. "Cast me not away from thy presence; and take not thy Holy Spirit from me." (Psalm 51:11)

There is an additional possibility for preparation. It has been termed "the interior lesson." Imagine the scene you are meditating upon as though it were actually taking place in front of you. Place yourself, for instance, at the foot of the cross. This will prevent your mind from wandering the same way a cage restricts a bird. I recommend these things for beginners, Philothea. The more subtle methods are for later.

After the imagination has helped you prepare yourself, begin to meditate intellectually. Choose a subject and begin to follow the thoughts as I have suggested. If a particular thought catches your interest, stay with it. The bees do not flit from flower to flower. They stay until they have gathered all the honey they can from each. If you find nothing for you after trying a particular thought, move on to the next. But don't rush the process. Take your time.

Meditation will naturally make you feel love of God and neighbor, as well as compassion, joy, sorrow, fear, confidence and the like. Go ahead and let it happen. But don't stop with such generalized responses. Change them into specific resolutions. For instance, you may be meditating upon our Lord's first word from the cross. This will certainly move you to forgive your personal enemies. But that is a small thing unless you go on to say, "Next time, I won't let _____ bother me so much. I will do everything I can to win that person's love." This will help you correct your faults quickly, Philothea. Without that specific last step, your progress will be much slower.

Conclude your meditation with humble thanks and an offering of yourself to God. Offer prayers and then gather a devotional nosegay. Let me explain what I mean by that. When people have been strolling through a beautiful garden they usually pick four or five flowers to take with them through the day. They smell them from time to time to cleanse their nostrils of foul odors. When our souls have roamed in meditation through a spiritual garden, we can choose two or three ideas that seemed most helpful and think about them occasionally all day long.

After your time of meditation, immediately begin to put into practice the resolutions you have made. Don't wait another day to get started. Without this application, meditation may be useless or even detrimental. Meditate on a virtue without practicing it and you will mislead yourself into believing that you have actually become someone you are not. If I have resolved to win the heart of my enemy by being gentle toward that person, I will try to find a way this very day to be friendly to him. If I am not able to see that person face-to-face, I will at least pray for him.

When your silent prayer is over, remain still and quiet for a few moments. Make your transition to other responsibilities gradually. Linger yet a while in the garden. Walk carefully along the path through the gate so that you won't spill the precious balm you are carrying. Don't be unnatural around other people, but keep as much prayer in you as you can.

There is an art to making the transition from prayer to earning a living. A lawyer must go from prayer to the courtroom, the merchant to his store, a homemaker to her responsibilities with a gentle motion that will not cause distress. Both prayer and your other duties are gifts from God.

Suppose you are attracted to God as soon as you have gone through the preparation. Then abandon the method I have outlined. The Holy Spirit has already given you the thing you would be seeking in the thoughts. Eventually, the formal steps will blend into a spontaneous unity.

Perhaps there will be a time when you will not experience the pleasures of meditation. Don't let that bother you. In a time like that return to familiar spoken prayers. Tell God you are sorry and ask him to help you. The important thing is to persevere. God grants or withholds his favors as he will. Our responsibility is to continue in a devotional manner before him.

One of the best things you can do, Philothea, is to remember all during the day that God is with you. Birds can return to their nests and deer to their thickets. We can select a place near Christ where we can retreat momentarily during the course of our work. Remember to take a few moments inwardly even as you are busy at your occupation. A crowd of people around will not be able to intrude upon this private act. King David was busy with many responsibilities, and yet he often says in his Psalms, "I am always near you. You hold my right hand"* (Ps.

73:23), or "I am continually aware of the nearness of God. He is present and I am strong"* (Ps. 16:8), or "I always look to the Lord for help."* (Ps. 25:15)

We will not often be too busy to turn aside to God for an instant. In fact, we can present our souls to him a thousand times a day. Sprinkle a seasoning of short prayers on your daily living. If you see something beautiful, thank God for it. If you are aware of someone's need, ask God to help. St. Francis looked at a stream of water and prayed, "God's grace flows just as gently and sweetly as this brook." You can toss up many such prayers all day long. They will help you in your meditation and in your secular employment as well. Make a habit of it.

By all means, go to church. There is always more value for you in public worship than in any private act of devotion. Give reverent attention to sermons. Apply the words you hear. Don't let them fall on the floor; take them into your heart.

Philothea, let me give you one warning. There is a thin line between inspiration and temptation. When you feel inspired, listen calmly, lovingly, to the proposal. But before you give your consent regarding any significant or extraordinary divine suggestion, be certain to ask your spiritual director's opinion. It may be that the enemy has observed your receptive attitude and has taken advantage of his opportunity.

III.

[The third part of the *Introduction* is much longer than the others. It consists of a series of lessons on virtuous behavior. Some of the topics may seem rather quaint to modern readers. Advice is given on a Christian's relationship to card playing, dancing, clothes, language, gambling, widowhood and virginity. While some readers may feel that the advice belongs in a museum, it must still be conceded that the writer is telling the truth, and that his assessment of the gains and losses in each case is accurate. For instance, there is no way we can take issue with this: "The only pleasure in gambling is winning, and that pleasure results from another's loss and pain. This is certainly evil." Or this: "Balls and dances are recreations that are morally neutral, but the manner in which they are conducted can push them toward hazardous evil." Limitations of space prevent a thorough rendering of this section, but the portion presented will give a fair sample of the whole.]

Some things people consider virtuous are not. I am thinking of ecstasies, rapturous insensibility, levitations, and similar magical stunts which are proffered as the highest spiritual experiences. Philothea, if these things happen they are not virtues; they are nothing more than gifts from God. It is not right for us to seek them. They are irrelevant to loving and serving God. If they come, they come from outside ourselves. All we are to try for is being good, devout men and women. If it pleases God to grant us a moment of angelic perfection, then we shall be good angels. But in the meantime, let's live sincerely, humbly and devoutly. Let's live patiently, obediently, with tenderness toward our neighbors. Let's learn to put up with their imperfections. Let's desire no chief seats with God, but be glad to serve him in his kitchen or his pantry, to be his janitors or garbagemen. If later he wants us to serve on his private cabinet, so be it. But God does not reward his servants in relation to the dignity of their positions, but in relation to the love and humility they bring to their assigned tasks.

Frankly, ecstatic religious experience is highly subject to make-believe, artificial pretensions. Many who think they are angels are not even good people. They talk higher than they live. If you are awestruck by another's holiness, remain content with your own lower and safer experience.

People can become proud and arrogant because they ride a handsome horse, or have a feather in their hat, or wear well-tailored clothes. If there is any glory in such things it surely belongs to the horse, the bird, and the tailor! Others are proud of their moustache, hair, bodies, ability to dance, play cards, or sing. This is utter frivolity! There are those who want to be respected because of their education, as though they automatically become everyone's teacher!

You can spot genuine goodness the same way you can identify the best balm. If it sinks to the bottom of a container of water and stays there, it is the most valuable balm. A truly wise, learned, generous, noble person will tend to be humble, modest, and eager to help another. If they float on the surface and show off, they are phonies. They are less genuine in direct proportion to their personal display.

Honors, titles, and rank are like saffron. Saffron grows best when it gets walked on. Honor is excellent when it is freely given to us by others, but it becomes cheap and degrading when we go looking for it. Beautiful flowers wither when plucked. Generous minds waste no time on such toys as rank or honor. They are occupied with other things. The owner of pearls pays no attention to shells.

On the other hand, Philothea, don't make a pretense of being humble. My advice is that you should never talk about it, and by all means never ask to be given the lowest place if you only mean to start there and work your way to the top.

Trust God's providence, but cooperate with him. Be like a little child who holds his father's hand while picking strawberries or blackberries in the hedgerows. If you must deal with the world's commerce with one hand, keep the other one with God. Look up to him now and then to see if he approves of what you are doing. Never think that you will be able to gather more if you use both hands. He is your success. Let go of him and you are in peril.

What I am getting at, Philothea, is that if your business is common enough, look at God rather than at it. If it becomes complicated and demands all of your attention, then still look now and then at God, the way sailors look at the sky rather than the water. This way God will work with you, in you, and for you.

IV.

Once it becomes evident that you intend to live a devout life, secular people will laugh at you and criticize you. The worst of them will say that because of some hard experiences you have run to God as an escape. Your friends will warn you of the unhappy consequences of your choice, saying that you will lose your reputation, become difficult to work with, or age prematurely. They will tell you that if you are going to live in the world, you must be a part of the world. They will call you an extremist and urge moderation upon you.

These foolish babblers are not concerned about you, Philothea. "If ye were of the world, the world would love his own; but because ye are not of the world, but I have chosen you out of the world, therefore the world hateth you." (John 15:19) Let some throw away many nights playing chess or cards and no one says anything about it. But if we give an hour to meditation they are ready to go for the doctor to cure us of our illness. The world is a biased judge, approving its own and dealing harshly with the children of God.

While light is a good thing, it can blind us after we have been in the dark. The change in your style of life, Philothea, may create some problems. Be patient. The strangeness will eventually wear off. To help you through some of the rough places, I will prepare you to deal with temptation, anxiety, and sadness.

Temptation

There is a vast difference between being tempted and yielding to it. And yet, if I know in advance that certain places will tempt me and I go there anyway, I am guilty of each temptation that comes my way.

The way to deal with temptations is to look away from them and at the Lord. Be certain you tell your spiritual director about them. If you are still subject to the temptations, continue to resist. There is no sin as long as you say, "No."

For every great temptation there will be many small ones. Wolves and bears are more dangerous than flies, but we are bothered most by the latter. You may never murder anyone, but you will certainly become angry. You may avoid adultery, but it is not easy to control your eyes. You may never steal anything from your neighbor, but you may covet it.

Let these flies and gnats buzz around you. Instead of fighting with them, do the very opposite of what the temptation is suggesting. For instance, if you are tempted to be vain, think about the troubles of others. If you are greedy, remember how death will take it all away from you and then go give something away or pass up a profit. Make the effort and you will be hardened against future temptations.

Anxiety

After sin, anxiety is the worst thing that can afflict a soul. It is the result of a strong desire to escape a present evil or to reach a desired goal. But anxiety increases the pain and prevents the attainment. Birds that are caught in nets flap and flutter wildly in an effort to escape, but only become more thoroughly trapped. When you want to get out of a bad situation and go to a good one, be sure you are calm and deliberate. I am not recommending carelessness, but an unhurried, untroubled approach to solving your problems. Without this, you may make a mess of things and have even more difficulty.

At the first sign of anxiety, pray to God. Talk with your spiritual director or some other friend. Sharing your grief unburdens your soul. It is the best remedy for anxiety.

Sadness

"God can use sadness to save us by changing our hearts. Wonderful! But common human sorrow is deadly."* (2 Cor. 7:10) Sadness, then, is both a blessing and a curse. It has many negative effects, but only two positive effects—compassion for others and repentance.

"Is any among you afflicted? Let him pray." (James 5:13) It is also helpful to get busy with some diverting work. Get around spiritual people and talk out your feelings with them. Keep trusting God. After this trial he will deliver you from evil.

Each day is unique. There are cloudy days and sunny; wet days and dry; windy days and calm. The seasons roll by as day turns into night and night into day. This variety makes beauty. And so it is with your life. There are ups and downs and no two days, no two hours, are ever exactly alike. A compass needle always points north regardless of the ship's course. If we will aspire toward God, the confusing changes of life will not unsteady us. "For whether we live, we live unto the Lord; and whether we die, we die unto the Lord: whether we live therefore, or die, we are the Lord's." (Rom. 14:8) Nothing can separate us from God's love. When little bees are caught in a storm they take hold of small stones so that they can keep their balance when they fly. Our firm resolution to stay with God is like ballast to the soul amid the rolling waves of life.

V.

If birds stop beating their wings, they quickly fall to the ground. Unless your soul works at holding itself up, your flesh will drag it down. Therefore, you must renew your determination regularly. Oddly, a spiritual crash leaves us lower than when we began. Clocks need winding, cleaning and oiling. Sometimes they need repair. Similarly, we must care for our spiritual life by examining and servicing our hearts at least annually.

[Helpful instructions are given regarding the conduct of such an annual check-up. The process of examining our various passions and behavior is compared to the lute player plucking each string in an effort to tune his instrument. Strong images and ideas nail down the recommitment to live the devout life.]

The world will object, Philothea, that I have told you to do so much that you will never have time for anything else. But I have not asked you to do it all every day. There will be plenty of time for the other things of life.

Three Final Instructions

1. Repeat your resolution to live the devout life on the first day of each month.

2. Admit openly that this is your desire. Don't say that you are devout; say you *want to be* devout. Feel no shame about this. If someone tells you that you can live a devout life without going through everything I have described, don't argue about it. Gently reply that you are weak and require more guidance than others.

3. Stay with it, Philothea. Time flies away. Keep your eyes on heaven. Don't throw it away for earth or the things of hell. Look at Jesus Christ and be faithful to him.

Live, Jesus! to whom, with the Father and the Holy Spirit, be all honor and glory, now and forevermore. Amen.

SUGGESTED ADDITIONAL READING

ST. AUGUSTINE

Augustine, St., *The Confessions of St. Augustine*. Trans. Albert C. Out-
ler. Philadelphia: Westminster, 1955.
————*The Confessions of St. Augustine*. Trans. John K. Ryan. Garden
City: Doubleday & Company, 1960.
————*The Confessions of St. Augustine*. Trans. F.J. Sheed. New York:
Sheed & Ward, 1943.
Marrou, Henri, *Saint Augustine and His Influence through the Ages*.
New York: Harper Torchbooks, 1957.
Smith, Warren Thomas, *Augustine: His Life and Thought*. Atlanta: John
Knox Press, 1980.

BERNARD OF CLAIRVAUX

Bernard of Clairvaux, St *The Works of Bernard of Clairvaux*. Cister-
cian Fathers Series, Number 13, Vol. 5. Washington, D.C.: Con-
sortium Press, 1974.
————*On the Song of Songs*. Trans. and ed. by a Religious of
C.S.M.V. London: A.R. Mowbray & Co., 1952. (See also num-
bers 4 & 7 in the Cistercian Fathers Series.)
————*Five Books on Consideration*. Cistercian Fathers Series, Number
37, Vol. 13. Kalamazoo, Michigan: Cistercian Publications, 1976.
Daniel-Rops, Henri. *Bernard of Clairvaux*. Trans. Elizabeth Abbot.
New York: Hawthorne, 1964.
Gilson, Etienne. *The Mystical Theology of Saint Bernard*. Trans.
A.H.C. Downes. New York: Sheed and Ward, 1939.

FRANCIS OF ASSISI

Chesterton, G.K., *St. Francis of Assisi*. Garden City: Doubleday & Company, 1924. (Reprinted as Image paperback, 1957.)

Jorgensen, Johannes, *St. Francis of Assisi*. Trans. T. O'Conor Sloane. Garden City: Doubleday & Company, 1955.

The Little Flowers of St. Francis. Trans. and ed. Raphael Brown. Garden City: Doubleday & Company, 1958.

BROTHER LAWRENCE

Lawrence, Brother, *The Practice of the Presence of God*. Trans. Donald Attwater. Springfield: Templegate, 1974.

————*The Practice of the Presence of God*. Spiritual Masters Series. New York/Ramsey: Paulist Press, 1978.

————*The Practice of the Presence of God*. Trans. E.M. Blaiklock. Nashville: Thomas Nelson, 1982.

————*The Practice of the Presence of God*. Trans. John J. Delaney. Garden City: Doubleday, 1977.

TERESA OF AVILA

Teresa of Avila, *The Interior Castle*. Trans. Kavanaugh & Rodriguez, The Classics of Western Spirituality Series. New York/Ramsey/Toronto: Paulist Press, 1979.

————*The Complete Works of St. Teresa of Jesus*. Trans. and ed. E. Allison Peers. New York: Sheed and Ward, 1946.

(Individual titles of the above have been reprinted by Doubleday in its Image Book Series. In addition to *Interior Castle*, *The Life of Teresa of Jesus* is recommended.)

FRANCOIS DE FÉNELON

Davis, James Herbert, Jr. *Fénelon*. Twayne's World Authors Series, Number 542. Boston: Twayne Publishers, 1979.

Fénelon, Francois de, *Christian Perfection*. Trans. and ed. Mildred Stillman. New York: Harper & Brothers, 1947 (Reis. Bethany, 1976).

————*Fénelon's Letters to Men and Women*. Trans. and ed. Derek Stanford. London: Peter Owens Ltd., 1957.

————*Meditations and Devotions*. Trans. and ed. Elizabeth Hassard. New York: P. O'Shea, 1864.

Little, Katharine Day, *François de Fénelon—A Study of a Personality*. New York: Harper & Brothers, 1951.

FRANCIS DE SALES

Camus, Jean Pierre, *The Spirit of Saint Francis de Sales*. Trans. C.F. Kelly. New York: Harper and Brothers, 1952.

Francis de Sales, *Introduction to the Devout Life*. Trans. John K. Ryan. Garden City: Doubleday, 1950 (Image Books, 1972).

————*On the Love of God*. Trans. John K. Ryan. Garden City: Doubleday & Co., 1963.